Passport's Illu

JAMAICA

FROM
THOMAS COOK

PASSPORT BOOKS
a division of *NTC Publishing Group*
Lincolnwood, Illinois USA

Published by Passport Books,
a division of NTC Publishing Group,
4255 W. Touhy Avenue,
Lincolnwood (Chicago), Illinois
60646–1975 U.S.A.

Written by Christopher P. Baker

Original photography by Jon Wyand

Edited, designed, and produced by AA Publishing.
© The Automobile Association 1995.
Maps © The Automobile Association 1995.

Library of Congress Catalog Card Number: 95-67007

ISBN 0-8442-9092-0

The contents of this publication are believed correct at the time of
printing. Nevertheless the publishers cannot accept responsibility for any
errors or omissions, for changes in the details given in this guide, or for
the consequences of any reliance on the information provided by the
same. Assessments of attractions, hotels, restaurants, and so forth are
based upon the author's own experience and therefore descriptions given
in this guide necessarily contain an element of subjective opinion that
may not reflect the publisher's opinion or dictate a reader's own
experiences on another occasion.
**We have tried to ensure accuracy in this guide, but things do
change and we would be grateful if readers would advise us of any
inaccuracies they may encounter.**

Published by AA Publishing (a trading name of Automobile Association
Developments Limited, whose registered office is Norfolk House,
Priestley Road, Basingstoke, Hampshire RG24 9NY. Registered number
1878835) and the Thomas Cook Group Ltd.

Published by Passport Books in conjunction with AA Publishing and the
Thomas Cook Group Ltd.

Color separation: BTB Colour Reproduction, Whitchurch, Hampshire,
England.

Printed by: Edicoes ASA, Oporto, Portugal.

Contents

About this Book

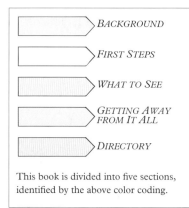

BACKGROUND

FIRST STEPS

WHAT TO SEE

GETTING AWAY FROM IT ALL

DIRECTORY

This book is divided into five sections, identified by the above color coding.

Treasure Beach: a great place to get away from it all

Background gives an introduction to Jamaica and its environs – its history, geography, politics, culture.

First Steps provides practical advice on arriving and getting around.

What to See is an alphabetical listing of places to visit, interspersed with walks and tours.

Getting Away from It All highlights places off the beaten track where it's possible to enjoy peace and quiet.

Directory provides practical information – from shopping and entertainment to children and sports, including a section on business matters. Special highly illustrated features on specific aspects of Jamaica appear throughout the book.

BACKGROUND

It is the fairest island that eyes have
beheld; mountainous . . . all full of
valleys and fields and plains.
CHRISTOPHER COLUMBUS
1494

Introduction

Since Columbus chanced upon Jamaica 500 years ago, millions of visitors have discovered that it surely is "the fairest island that eyes have beheld." The Caribbean's third-largest island looks as if it were spawned from its own picture postcard.

Here Mother Nature has concentrated all the splendors she elsewhere sows parsimoniously throughout the tropics: cascading waterfalls, lush green mountains, ribbons of talcum-fine sand, the rustle of trade winds teasing the palms, and flowers that spill their petals everywhere.

JAMAICA LOCATOR

through green canyons or a horseback ride in the cool Blue Mountains. Play golf, climb a waterfall, tour a haunted mansion, explore a once sinful pirate city, picnic on an old colonial sugar plantation, or visit a museum to learn about Jamaica's brutal slave-era history.

Much of Jamaica is still engaged in survival. Kingston, the capital city and a

After a dark northern winter and the turmoils of a northern lifestyle, Jamaica soothes like a pleasant dream. You sense it the moment you arrive and are greeted by two of the very things you came to enjoy – fabulous sunny weather and the murmur of surf echoing across a sea as warm and as flat as bedtime milk.

You can, if you wish, spend your days being lulled to sleep on the beach by the whisper of waves. You can also whisk across the bright turquoise shallows on a windsurfer, sunfish, or water-skis; or head out into the cobalt-blue sea to snorkel, dive, or try your hand at deep-sea game fishing. Away from the shore, Jamaica tickles every tastebud – there is so much to see and do it is difficult to know where to start. Take a romantic raft ride

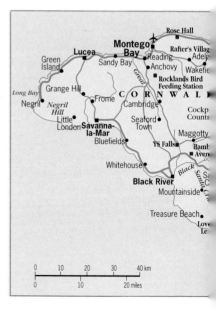

major cultural center, is marred by ghettos where drug wars are fought. Poverty gnaws at the very edges of tourist resorts. Although this *grande dame* of the English-speaking Caribbean has weathered economic hard times in recent years, the enchanting tropical beauty seems to wash away worries.

Jamaica's vibrant local culture is intense, complex, and exciting. Reggae and Rastafarians, zesty cuisine and piquant patois are as much a part of the Jamaican experience as its natural beauty and fascinating history.

Add the widest selection of accommodations in the Caribbean – luxury hotels, thatched cottages by the sea, economical villas, and fabulous all-inclusive resorts – and you have the recipe for a holiday guaranteed to make you forget the worries of the workaday world.

A customer at Black River Market

JAMAICA

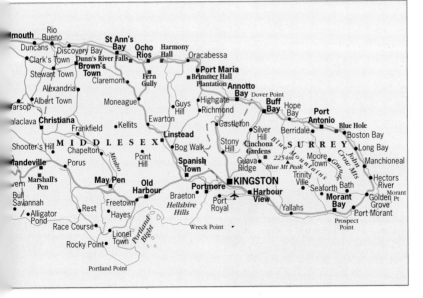

Geography

*J*amaica, which floats in the Caribbean sea 18 degrees north of the Equator, is 146 miles long, with widths varying between 22 and 51 miles. At 4,244 square miles, it is roughly the size of Connecticut or half that of Wales. It has such acute variations in scenery, climate, and character, however, that it is truly a world in one island.

LANDSCAPE

The name Jamaica derives from the Arawak Indian word for their island, Xaymaca: "land of wood and water." And so it is, with countless rivers and waterfalls flowing down from mountains swathed in forests of aqueous green. The scalloped coastal plains and deeply incised central highlands are ripe with emerald meadows and fields of lime-green sugarcane-like sheets of green silk. The broad southern plain, however, in parts resembles the African savanna; it even has cactus and, in contrast, Everglades-like swamp. The beaches that sparkle for mile upon mile have their own contrasts – white sand in the west and north, black sand in the south.

GEOLOGY

Volcanic forces began to push the island up from the sea 30 million years ago – the limestone that covers two-thirds of Jamaica was once seabed. The island is still rising and earthquakes are common. A series of mountains form the island's spine, soaring to 7,402 feet at Blue Mountain Peak in the east, and almost half of Jamaica lies above 1,000 feet. The limestone plateaus – typified by the Cockpit Country – are pitted with depressions, sinkholes, and stygian chambers. A sprawling coral reef protects the north shore from breakers that chew at the cliffs on the eastern coast.

FLORA AND FAUNA

This lush Eden lies buried under almost 3,000 species of plants (800 indigenous), including 200 orchid, 60 bromeliad, and 550 fern species. In the Blue Mountains, bamboo, rhododendron, and stunted dwarf forest are haunted by mists. Cactus rise from the parched earth of the south. Many of the fruit species were introduced: Breadfruit was brought from the South Seas by Captain Bligh, coconut came from Malaysia, and ackee from Africa. Pimento is native, as is guava, pineapple, soursop and cedar, ebony, and lignum vitae.

Mongooses are commonly seen. They

This verdant scene is just one of the many varied landscapes of Jamaica

HURRICANES

In midsummer, northeast and southeast trade winds merge near the equator, spawning high-pressure squalls that centrifugal forces can whip into hurricanes. Winds can reach 120 mph. Jamaica has been hit by westward-moving hurricanes on several occasions, most recently by Hurricane Gilbert in September 1988. The hurricane season is between August and October.

HURRICANE GILBERT

Everywhere you travel in Jamaica you'll hear tales of Hurricane Gilbert. The tropical cyclone struck the island a knock-out blow on 12 September 1988 when it came ashore near Port Antonio. Gilbert's 150 to 185 mph winds followed Jamaica's longitudinal axis, cutting a swathe of devastation across the entire island.

Agriculture suffered immeasurably: Entire crops – coffee, cocoa, sugarcane, bananas – were lost. Many businesses remained idle for months while Kingston and much of Jamaica were without electricity. And community life was severely disrupted: Roads were washed out and thousands of homes were destroyed, as were hospitals, schools, public buildings, botanical gardens, and several tourist attractions.

were introduced to control rats, but they also decimated the native coney (a large guinea-pigish creature) and snakes (all harmless). There are twenty-five species of bats. Manatees, the tuskless walrus-like creatures that inspired tales of mermaids, survive along the south coast alongside American crocodiles (called alligators in Jamaica). Jamaica's avifauna includes hummingbirds, parrots, and todies (see **Birds** of Jamaica, pages 80–1).

CLIMATE

Sun and trade winds bestow near-perfect weather. Temperatures seldom vary, averaging 82 °F year round on the coast. The "Doctor Breeze" helps keep you cool. The mountainous interior is crisper – cool and less humid—and in the Blue Mountains locals sometimes light fires to keep warm. Midsummer (May–October) brings the bulk of the rain. Moisture-laden trade winds spill most of their rain on the mountains – a rain shadow for the relatively parched southern plains. The northeast is Jamaica's rainy corner.

POPULATION

Approximately 2.5 million people live on Jamaica, primarily of African origin, with minorities of European, East Indian, and Chinese. Towns and cities contain 46 percent of the population, with one-third of the island's population in Kingston.

ECONOMY

Jamaica is poor. It faces a huge foreign debt and has twenty-five percent unemployment. Tourism is the leading industry, generating $860 million in 1993. Bauxite, the mainstay of the economy in the 1960s and 1970s, today accounts for about forty percent of exports. Sugarcane dominates agriculture and remains the island's largest employer, while bananas, coffee, and cocoa are key exports. Manufacturing is led by textiles, footwear, and food and beverage industries. Illegal ganja (marijuana) sales generate an estimated $1 billion dollars annually.

History

c AD650

Arawak Indians from the Orinoco region of South America arrive and settle the island they call Xaymaca ("Land of wood and water").

c1400

The Arawak's peaceful existence is upset by the arrival of fierce Caribs, a cannibalistic Indian tribe from the Guiana region of South America

1491

Columbus anchors at St Ann's Bay during his second voyage to the New World. He names the island St Jago, or Santiago, after St James.

1503–4

Columbus returns during his fourth voyage, runs aground near St Ann's Bay, and is stranded for a full year.

1510

The Spaniards establish the colony of Seville Nueva and begin enslaving the peaceful, sea-going Arawak Indians, who had occupied Xaymaca since about AD650. The Arawak population of perhaps 100,000 is reduced within 150 years to less than 100.

1517

The first enslaved Africans arrive in Jamaica. For the next century the island remains little more than a supply base for Spain's other colonies.

1534

Sevilla Nueva is abandoned. A new capital is established at San Jago de la Vega (today's Spanish Town).

1655

A British fleet sails into Kingston harbor and captures Jamaica. The Spanish are allowed to escape to Cuba. They release their slaves, who flee to the hills and form the Maroons.

1658

The Spanish attempt to seize back Jamaica and are defeated at the Battle of the Rio Nuevo. British colonize the island as part of Oliver Cromwell's Western Design – a grandiose scheme for expanding England's holdings in the Caribbean at the expense of Spain's.

1660s

Governor Thomas Modyford gives buccaneers royal protection to harass Spanish colonies and ships. Port Royal grows wealthy and earns the nickname "the wickedest city in the world."

1670

Jamaica is formally ceded to Britain by the Treaty of Madrid.

1690

Slaves rebel throughout the island. British authorities respond brutally. Clarendon slaves, led by Cudjoe, ally with the Maroons and launch the First Maroon War.

1692

Port Royal is destroyed by an earthquake. The Jamaican government begins crack-down on buccaneering.

1694

A French fleet under Admiral du Casse invades Jamaica and destroys over fifty sugar plantations but is defeated at Carlisle Bay.

1739

The Maroons sign treaty with the British and are given land and self-government. The Maroons agree to capture runaway slaves and to assist in suppressing rebellions and invasions.

1760

A Coromantee slave rebellion in the Port Maria area spreads throughout the island. The Maroons help suppress it.

1795

The Second Maroon War breaks out when two Trelawny Maroons are flogged for stealing pigs. British troops import bloodhounds to hunt Maroons, who eventually sue for peace. More than 600 Maroons are deported to Canada, and then to Sierra Leone, becoming the first Africans repatriated from the New World.

1807

Britain abolishes slave trade to British colonies.

1831

The Black preacher "Daddy" Sam Sharpe leads a Christmas slave rebellion around Montego Bay. Severe retribution by authorities fuels antislavery sentiment in England.

1834

The British parliament passes an Act abolishing slavery. In 1838 Britain pays compensation to Jamaican slaveholders, and slavery finally ends in Jamaica. Indentured laborers are imported from India.

1865

The Morant Bay Rebellion, led by black deacon Paul Bogle, is savagely repressed by the governor, who executes 430 "conspirators" Parliament recalls the governor and makes Jamaica a British Crown Colony.

1872

The capital of Jamaica is moved from Spanish Town to Kingston.

1907

Much of Kingston is destroyed by a great earthquake, which claims more than 800 lives.

The new street plan remains the basis for the city's layout today.

1938

Social disaffection fosters widespread violence and riots. Alexander Bustamante organizes Jamaica's first officially recognized labor union. The People's National Party is later founded by socialist Norman Manley.

1944

New constitution grants universal adult suffrage. Jamaica becomes fully self-governing based on the British model of a bicameral parliament.

1962

Jamaica is granted independence, with Sir Alexander Bustamente as its first prime minister. The British monarch remains head of state, represented by a governor-general. Jamaica enters the Commonwealth of Nations.

1972

PNP wins election. Michael Manley becomes prime minister, ushering in a period of leftist reform that generates economic instability. Subsequent elections marred by violence.

1980

JLP (Jamaican Labour Party) wins election. Manley is succeeded by Edward Seaga, who returns Jamaica to a more moderate economic and political path. Hundreds of people are killed during waves of election violence.

1988

Hurricane Gilbert devastates the island. Thousands of homes are destroyed.

Statue of Columbus
at St Ann's

SLAVERY

The Spaniards imposed their culture with the musket ball; the English imposed theirs with the chain and whip. Thus is Jamaica's history writ – painfully, as a slave colony.

From their earliest days the Spanish colonists enslaved the indigenous Arawak population. Within a few decades the Indians were decimated, and African slaves were imported to replace them.

The English, who captured the island from Spain in 1655, swiftly developed Jamaica as a sugar economy, and huge fortunes were amassed by the cane planters (a new phrase came into British parlance: "as wealthy as a West Indian planter"). The plantocracy established plantations throughout the island, and, to support the bustling estates, the British brought in thousands of African slaves. By the late 18th century Jamaica had become a center of the slave trade in the Western Hemisphere, with a population composed of about 300,000 black slaves and 20,000 whites.

Almost one in five Africans died during the Middle Passage – the horror-

Heb. 5. 15.

PHŒBE.

Jamaica Royal Gazette, Oct. 7, 1826.

Spanish-Town Workhouse.

35—42

Notice is hereby given, that unless the undermentioned Slave is taken out of this Workhouse, prior to Monday the 30th day of October next, she will on that day, between the hours of 10 and 12 o'Clock in the forenoon, be put up to Public Sale, and sold to the highest and best bidder, at the Cross-Keys Tavern, in this Town, agreeably to the Workhouse Law now in force, for payment of her fees.

PHŒBE, a Creole, 5 feet 4½ inches, marked NELSON on breasts, and I O on right shoulder, first said to one Miss Robert, a free Black, in Vere, secondly, to Thomas Oliver, Esq. St. John's, but it is very lately ascertained that her right name is Quashel, and she belongs to Salisbury-Plain plantation, in St. Andrew's. Mr. John Smith is proprietor.   May

Ordered, that the above be published in the Newspapers a pointed by Law, for Eight Weeks.

By order of the Commissioners,

T. RENNALLS, Sup

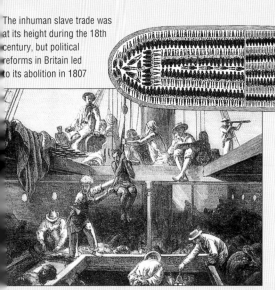

The inhuman slave trade was at its height during the 18th century, but political reforms in Britain led to its abolition in 1807

branded and commonly flayed, burned alive, and otherwise brutally tortured.

The excesses were gradually controlled through Acts of Parliament, but the backbreaking field work and severity of life took its toll. Mortality was so great that six slaves died for each birth on the island. Over 600,000 slaves were imported to Jamaica between 1700 and 1807, when the trade was abolished. Yet the slave population was only 250,000 in 1834, the year of emancipation.

filled voyage across the Atlantic – when slaves were chained head-to-toe in the putrid bowels of slave ships. Less than half lived to be put to work in the fields.

The white plantocracy ran their estates through tyranny. Slaves were

Not surprisingly, slave uprisings were common. The plantocracy lived in fear of their lives, and rebellions were put down with brutal severity. The success of the slave revolt in Haiti in 1798 inspired slave revolts throughout the Caribbean.

In December 1831 a Baptist preacher named Sam Sharpe led 20,000 slaves in gaining control of a plantation near Montego Bay. The English quashed the revolt by announcing that parliament had abolished slavery. In vengeful retribution, more than 1,000 slaves were executed. "Daddy" Sharpe was hanged in the Montego Bay square that today bears his name.

The severity of the punishment helped force the passage of the 1834 law abolishing slavery throughout the British empire.

Politics

*J*amaica borrows heavily from the British political stage in tradition and institution. The island is one of the Caribbean's oldest and most stable democracies. Nevertheless, it lends singular, often unbridled, partisan passions to the scene, and political violence at election time commonly makes worldwide news.

Constitution

Jamaica is an independent state and a member of the British Commonwealth of Nations. Under the 1962 Constitution the queen of England is head of state (the queen of Jamaica), represented by a governor-general whose functions are mostly ceremonial. The governor-general is appointed on the recommendation of the Jamaican prime minister.

The island is also a parliamentary democracy. Political power is vested in parliament, a bicameral body consisting of a House of Representatives with sixty members and a Senate with twenty-one members. The representatives are elected by a simple majority in their constituencies. The prime minister appoints thirteen members of the Senate; the remainder are appointed by the leader of the opposition.

National elections are held every five years, and all

The Jamaican flag

nationals over 18 have the right to vote if they have registered. The leader of the political party that wins a simple majority becomes prime minister.

Local government

Jamaica is divided into fourteen parishes, each run by an elected council. The parishes of Kingston and St Andrew together form the Kingston Metropolitan Area. The senior justice of the peace (judge) holds the ceremonial position of Custos Rotulorum, the queen's representative for each parish. The three counties (Cornwall, Middlesex, and Surrey) no longer have a political function.

Political parties

Two major political parties dominate the scene and have alternated in power since the first national election in 1944.

The People's National Party (PNP) espouses "democratic socialism." It was formed in 1938 by barrister Norman Manley (Bustamante's cousin). Manley was succeeded as leader of the PNP in 1969 by his son Michael, a journalist and trade unionist who as prime minister (1972–80) adopted a progressive yet controversial leftist domestic policy and a "non-aligned" international policy.

When re-elected in 1989 Manley went from anti American firebrand to middle-of-the-road tourism promoter. He resigned due to ill health in 1992.

All quiet now, but tempers can flare at election time in Jamaica

The party is presently headed by lawyer and current prime minister Percival J Patterson, a moderate who won a landslide election victory in 1993. Patterson is the nation's first black prime minister.

The Jamaica Labour Party (JLP) was formed in 1943 by labor leader Alexander Bustamente. Despite its name, the JLP is essentially a pro-business, conservative party. It is headed by Edward Seaga, who as prime minister (1980–9) attempted to revive a collapsed economy. The PNP boycotted the 1983 elections and Seaga basically ran a one-party state until 1989. His policies are generally accepted as having succeeded in rekindling the economy, despite worsening poverty for the majority of Jamaicans. The social distress cost him the 1989 election.

The leftist Workers Party of Jamaica and rightist Jamaica America Party are the leading lesser political parties.

POLITICAL VIOLENCE

Patronage dominates Jamaican politics (the winning party usually rewards loyal supporters with political positions, contracts, etc.), thereby creating vested interests and deepening existing passions. In 1976 the political polarization boiled over in the ghettos of Kingston, where militant party supporters enforce their political stranglehold through vigilantes. In 1980 the ghettos exploded. More than 700 died in battles between adherents of the PNP and JLP. Since then party leaders have sought to quell violence. In the 1989 and 1993 elections "only" twenty-five people were killed.

RASTAFARIANS

No visitor to Jamaica can fail to notice the Rastafarians (Rastas), with their red, gold, and green woollen tams and wildly tangled beards and hair. Jamaica's cultural rebels are often misunderstood. Despite their wild looks, Rastas live by a philosophy of peace and brotherly love.

Their prophet is Marcus Garvey (1887–1940), a Jamaican national hero and black rights advocate who in 1919 predicted the crowning of a black king – the Redeemer – in Africa. In 1930 Ras Tafari Makonnen (*Ras*, an honorific given to royalty; *tafari*, the family name) was crowned Emperor Haile Selassie of Ethiopia. Biblical references to support Selassie's divinity were touted, and a following emerged in Jamaica. Rastafarians consider Selassie to be a direct descendant of King Solomon and adopted Selassie's early name for themselves.

Rastas grow their hair without combing until it twists and mats into locks – dreadlocks – that may dangle below the waist. They are guided in this by the biblical passage, "They shall not make baldness upon their head, neither shall they shave off the corner of their beard. . . " (Leviticus 21:5).

A Rasta's whole life is a nonviolent protest against oppression. They believe themselves one of the lost tribes of Israel delivered into exile by the whites and left wandering in Babylon – Jamaica. Oppression is also "Babylon," as are authority figures and institutions: the police, government, and so on. One day God – Jah – is expected to lead them back to Ethiopia, their Promised Land, or Zion.

Traditionalist Rastas prefer to live a simple life in the country, away from the pollution of Babylon. The most ardent are vegetarians with fastidious taboos. They eat only *I-tal* – natural foods. They are also teetotallers and nonsmokers, despite their reverence for ganja (marijuana), which they consume copiously. Smoking ganja – "wisdom weed" or the "sacred herb" – is

considered a religious act and is often accompanied by recitations of prayers and psalms. A ganja pipe is known as a chalice and is ideally made of cow or goat horn (but usually wood).

Rastas take great pride in black history and artistic and athletic

Aspects of Rasta
life: hats
(above),
dreadlocks (left),
and the late Bob
Marley (right)

attainment while honoring codes against avarice, dishonesty, exploitation, and sexual envy. They eschew the Christian concept of redemption in favor of the concept of heaven in the here and now.

Jamaica's politicians often pay homage to Rastafarianism in recognition of its sway. The creed has also lent many colorful phrases to the Jamaican dialect: "one love," a parting expression meaning peace or unity, for example, and "cool runnings," a good-bye, blessing, and encouragement.

Culture

*J*amaica's proud motto is "out of many, one people." The island is a spectrum of races: Decades of intermarriage have produced features and shades of every color.

The vast majority of Jamaicans – ninety-five percent – are descendants of African slaves or their unions with European masters. (Black Jamaicans regard themselves as Jamaicans and like to be referred to as such, not as "natives" – a term that historically was used to connote primitive). Significant minorities, whose ancestors came from Lebanon, Germany, India, and China, stitched their identities on to the soul and sinew of Jamaican culture.

The island's savage history has imbued Jamaicans with a fierce independence and pride – traits they share with Anancy, a spider and folk hero who grapples with a harsh world by deviousness, sharp intelligence, and quick wit. Jamaicans are opinionated and often argumentative; but politeness and courtesy are also part of the national heritage. Jamaicans are quick to give and respond to a hearty "Good morning!" Above all they are friendly – and funny. Their deprecating sense of humor is subtle, sardonic, and often bawdy.

The average Jamaican dresses conservatively, but in other regards he or she is permissive. Casual sexual liaisons, for example, are common. Jamaican women are proudly independent and may typically have children by several men before marrying relatively late in life. Nevertheless, beside the beds of many Jamaicans lies the King James Version of the Bible. (The island has what feels like more churches per mile than any other country in the world!) The Anglican Church has the largest membership. Rastafarianism is another potent force (see pages 16–17), and African *pocomania* rites linger on.

The African heritage is deeply rooted in Jamaican song and dance. The rhythm of reggae, the heartbeat of the nation, owes much to the beat of the African drum. You will hear it all over the island, an elemental expression of joy in the face of hardship.

There's always time for the donkey to have a quick snack

FIRST STEPS

Get it together in Jamaica.
Soulful town, soulful people,
I see you're having fun.
Dancing to the reggae rhythm.
Oh, island in the sun! Come on and
Smile, you're in Jamaica.
BOB MARLEY,
Smile Jamaica

First Steps

*J*amaica is all you expect—Glorious weather, superb beaches, reggae and rum, and scenic beauty that is unsurpassed. But then again, it is *not* what you expect. Misconceptions about Jamaica are rife. A little advance knowledge will better prepare you.

CRIME

Jamaica has a worldwide reputation for violent crime, spawned by political violence (mostly in Kingston) during the late 1970s. The negative publicity, however, has left an indelible image.

Actually Jamaica is much safer than many people think, but it must be recognized that muggings and opportunistic theft do occur, and that they have increased in recent years. In 1994, however, the Jamaican government introduced a sweeping anti-crime initiative in major resort towns (see also **Crime** in the **Practical Guide**).

Take the same precautions you would in any unfamiliar destination. Always leave any valuables in your hotel safe and do not wear jewelry. Carry no more money than you need, use money belts, and keep wallets out of view. Avoid walking in poorly lit streets or on remote beaches at night. And avoid Kingston's violent ghettos, where gun battles are fought over drug wars and politics.

DRIVING

Main highways are generally well paved. However, the road that skirts the east coast, and secondary roads that wind inland, go from tarmac to pebbles and then to mud. High in the mountains roads are often reduced to what amounts to a set of stairs that your car ascends with difficulty.

Rural Jamaicans refer to precipitous paths hacked out of steep hillsides as "roads." Roads that are passable for vehicles are called "drivin' roads."

Jamaicans drive on the left. Remember the local saying: "The left side is the right side. The right side is suicide!"

Jamaicans are fast drivers. They like to pass and are often reckless in doing so. Jamaican drivers are not particularly courteous (they're often argumentative and will even stop to hurl abuse at drivers who cross them). They often creep through red lights or disregard them altogether, so be particularly careful at intersections.

Watch for people, as well as goats and

Skilled hands shape a dug-out canoe from cottonwood at Port Antonio

Mandeville – a dreadlocked vendor of sugarcane

cattle, wandering on the road; and pay particular attention to chickens, which often display suicidal urges that answer the question, "Why did the chicken cross the road?" (See also **Driving** in the **Practical Guide**).

FINDING YOUR FEET

Jamaica's poverty can come as a shock. Steel yourself! Also, prepare yourself for a much slower pace of life. Patience and good humor is required in restaurants and elsewhere. And adopt Jamaican time.

Do not be surprised, too, if you're called by such names as "whitey" (even if you're black – foreigners are lumped together). It is not derogatory. Such blunt terms are used merely as tags of identification. And do not take undue offense at what may appear to be arrogance: Jamaicans are often argumentative and opinionated without intended malice.

GANJA (MARIJUANA)

The chances are that you will not be in Jamaica long before someone offers you ganja – marijuana. The "sacred herb" was introduced in the 19th century by indentured laborers from India and has since become an integral part of Jamaican culture. To Rastafarians it is sacred – the staff of life.

Many Jamaicans depend on marijuana – "the poor man's friend" – for their income (St Ann, the "Garden Parish," is commonly called the "Ganga Parish"). It generates hundreds of millions of dollars a year in foreign exchange from illegal sales.

Beachside hagglers are likely to try to sell you some "smoke" – regardless of your age or appearance.

The possession and sale of drugs is strictly illegal, and offenders face strict punishment. Random road searches are common, and tourists are favorite targets.

Buses are cheap, but the driver will not leave until his vehicle is full

GETTING AROUND
The domestic airline, Trans-Jamaican, operates between Montego Bay, Ocho Rios, Port Antonio, Negril, and Kingston. Private small-plane charters can also be arranged. The rail service was discontinued in 1992.

The bus system is an adventure! It is a great way to meet the locals but is very disorganized, overcrowded, and it operates to no set timetable. Car rental charges can give you a shock, but there are plenty of companies to choose from (see the **Practical Guide** for more information).

HAGGLING
Bargaining – haggling – is a way of life. Prices in markets and from beach or roadside vendors are always negotiable. Regard shopping as a sport and you will have fun. Getting real bargains will thoroughly test your skills!

HUSTLERS
Jamaicans in popular tourist areas can be aggressive in their sales pitch. You will be pressured to buy unwanted items and to pay for unwanted services, real or imagined, and offers commonly include prostitution – by both men and women. If long-haired, you will be cajoled to have your hair braided. Or you may be asked to pay for a photograph innocently taken: "Jus' give sometin' for I, jus' a likkle."

Say "No!" – firmly, but in a friendly tone – then expect to say it again. The persistence can chafe, though it is not threatening. Beneath the pushiness is usually a warmth that can be drawn out by a smile.

LAY OF THE LAND
Montego Bay, on the northwest coast, is Jamaica's most convenient and popular resort, with fine beaches, an active nightlife, and a bustling city center.

Ocho Rios, a beautiful 90-minute drive east from Mo'Bay, follows a slower pace and is a node for a panoply of sightseeing excursions. This popular tourist resort is favored by cruise ships.

Port Antonio lies way to the east – a magnificent and occasionally white-knuckle drive over the Blue Mountains or around the south coast from Kingston. It is slightly down-at-heel but reclusive, up-scale resorts nestled in secluded coves.

Negril, Jamaica's westernmost outpost and self-proclaimed party town, is a 90-minute drive from Mo'Bay. It blends a stunning beach and fabulous watersports with a laid-back, anything-goes lifestyle.

Mandeville lies far from the madding crowds in the mountainous heart of Jamaica, a 2-hour drive south from Mo'Bay or Ocho Rios. The untramelled south coast lies within easy reach.

PATOIS

"Walk good" is not a grammatical error. It is a Jamaican saying and means "safe journey." The Queen's English is the official language, but Jamaica's unofficial lingo is the local *patois* – a linguistic frontier almost impenetrable by the visitor.

"Jamaican talk" twists the mother tongue, adds slang, and peppers it with Spanish, African, Irish, Welsh, and other words that have all found their way into the broth.

The result is often lewd and laconic. For "Mind your own business" there is "Cockroach no bizness in a fowl-yard"; for the pretentious there is "Monkey, the higher 'im climb, the more 'im expose." Instead of "I love you" a Jamaican paramour may say, "Girl, me luv you to det', free food and money forget." "Cool runnings" is patois for "good-bye" and

also a blessing. Two phrases you will hear often are "Irie" and "No problem." They mean everything is fine. Relax. Be cool.

Stay for just a few days and you will be talking Jamaican, too.

NUDE BATHING

Many tourists visit Jamaica to indulge in some full-body tanning. Jamaica is a permissive society and it is not uncommon to see village women bathing topless in rivers. However, many Jamaicans are deeply religious and easily offended by bare skin. Nude bathing should be restricted to designated areas only. Options include Navy Island in Port Antonio; Seawind Beach Resort in Montego Bay; Booby Cay, the northern end of Long Bay, and Hedonism II in Negril; and Sandals and Couples in Ocho Rios.

Not many customers just now at this shop in Hagley Gap

THE OTHER JAMAICA

Tourism has not completely taken over Jamaica – the island still holds the promise of mystery. It has beaches, but it also has bush. Away from the beach resorts an entirely different experience lies close at hand yet a world away, along roads that are portals to vibrant market towns and off-the-beaten-track villages (you should take advice before venturing too far on your own – some areas are not recommended). Here you can experience traditional life and discover that, despite Jamaica's lingering poverty, her smile is full-blossomed sincere, and bright.

> ### MEET THE PEOPLE
> The ideal way to learn about Jamaica is in the company of a Jamaican friend. The Jamaican Tourist Board's Meet the People program will match you up with a local person or family for an afternoon at the beach, a religious service, a picnic in the mountains, or a night of reggae. The governor and his wife might even invite you for tea! Almost 1,000 families are registered hosts. You spend as much time with your new Jamaican friends as you like. The program is free, and all expenses incurred are borne by the host (show your appreciation with a gift).

Bamboo Avenue, a two-mile glade of giant bamboos

WHEN TO GO

Jamaica has a balmy year-round climate. On the coast temperatures are always warm and vary only slightly (see **Climate**, page 9) with the seasons. The cooler, drier months are December to April; most salubrious of all is February and March. You will pay more for the pleasure, however – hotels charge higher prices during peak season.

If you do not mind extra rain, visit in May to October. September and October, the rainiest months, are a good time to visit the drier south coast.

Hotels and tour operators slash their rates from mid-April to mid-December, when a less-hurried pace prevails.

WHAT TO WEAR

Pack light, loose-fitting cotton garments. A sweater or light jacket is needed for the highlands and even some nights on the coast. What you wear to dinner will depend on where you are dining. Many up-market resorts and restaurants require jackets and ties for men, and dresses for women. Elsewhere, Jamaican formality merely means putting on shoes. Dress code for discos is simple – just throw on a T-shirt to ride de reggae riddims.

If you burn easily, pack long-sleeved shirts and long pants, plus sunhats. Tropical downpours can be sudden and heavy, and an umbrella is more practical than a raincoat.

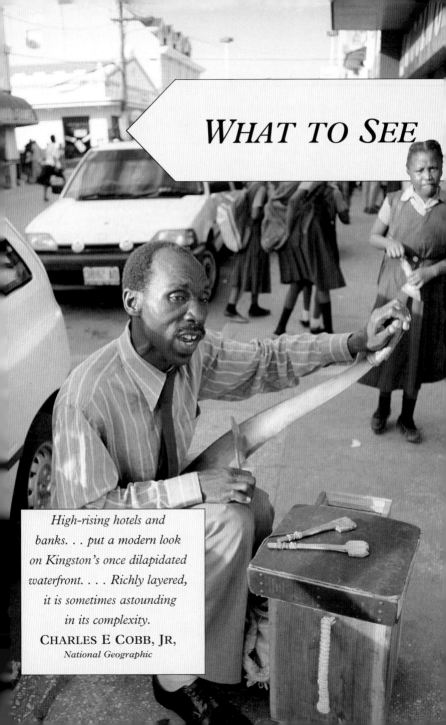

WHAT TO SEE

High-rising hotels and
banks. . . put a modern look
on Kingston's once dilapidated
waterfront. . . . Richly layered,
it is sometimes astounding
in its complexity.
CHARLES E COBB, JR,
National Geographic

Kingston

*C*ontrary to popular opinion, Kingston is not all, or even mostly, a ghetto. The metropolis – the largest English-speaking city south of Miami – is the intellectual center of Jamaica, as well as the cultural capital of the Caribbean. The richly layered city resonates with music, theater, and dance.

Kingston is also a perfect base for exploring the historic pirate haunt of Port Royal and the enchanting Blue Mountains.

Kingston, the nation's capital (population 800,000), is not a beautiful city, though its waterfront setting against the soaring Blue Mountains is dramatic. Its outskirts are surrounded by industry – bauxite, cement, oil, flour – and shacks no bigger than a one-car garage nailed together with planks and strips of tin. The bustle of energy grows as you close in on the city center.

Downtown, near the wharves of the world's seventh-largest natural harbor, is the oldest part of the city. Much of the

decent colonial architecture is here, including theaters that are venues for the Jamaica Philharmonic, the National Chorale, the Jamaican Folk Singers, and the widely acclaimed National Dance Theatre Company.

New Kingston, to the north, is a more relaxed region of high-rise offices, banks, insurance companies, and parks. It is anchored by Half Way Tree, a square where old and new Kingston meet. Hope Gardens, the island's foremost botanic gardens, is here. So too are Devon House, Kings House (home to the governor-general), Jamaica House (the prime minister's office), the University of the

A splendid sunset gives way to the lights of Kingston at dusk

West Indies, and a range of restaurants reflecting the world's best cuisines.

On the city outskirts are Caymanas Park (a venue for horse racing) and two 18-hole championship golf courses. Less than an hour away you can be thousands of feet up in the mountains, sampling coffee and the magnificent view, or exploring the remains of Port Royal, erstwhile pirate capital of the Caribbean, half an hour's drive away across the harbor. Near Port Royal are the Cays, uninhabited white-sand islands good for snorkeling and bathing.

Day and night, Kingston vibrates with reggae, the cool-hot musical phenomenon that was born in the ghettos and is sure to put a spring in your step (for an appreciation of reggae, stop in at the **Bob Marley Museum**). Avoid the ghettos, such as Trench Town, Beirut, and Falklands, which stretch for miles. Here "rude boys," or gang leaders, rule their territories with guns. Outsiders cannot enter without permission. Nor would you want to.

Thirty years ago Kingston was a mecca for tourists. The city authorities are making new efforts to convince today's travelers that it is a fascinating – and safe – place to visit.
For information contact the Jamaica Tourist Board (tel: (809) 929–9200) in the ICWI Building, 2 St Lucia Avenue, Kingston 5.

BOB MARLEY MUSEUM
The late Bob Marley's home and Tuff Gong recording studio is now a museum – the most visited site in Kingston – that chronicles his life from ghetto to reggae superstardom and premature death. A statue of Marley holding his guitar stands in front of the porticoed entrance.

Bob Marley's old home, now a museum

Hour-long tours lead you through the grounds and modestly decorated house containing Marley's gold and platinum records, Rastafarian religious cloaks, and other memorabilia. The old recording studio is now an exhibition hall and theater.

Outside, your guide will point out the tall shade tree beneath which Marley smoked ganja (marijuana), plus bulletholes in the rear of the house from an assassination attempt in 1976.
56 Hope Road, Kingston 6 (tel: (809) 927–9152). Open: Monday, Tuesday, Thursday, and Friday, 9:30am–4:30pm; Wednesday, Saturday, and public holidays, 12:30pm–5:30pm. Admission charge.

COIN AND NOTES MUSEUM
The history of Jamaican tokens, coins, and paper money is told in this tiny museum. Guided tours are offered.
Bank of Jamaica Building, Ocean Boulevard, Kingston 1 (tel: (809) 922–0750). Open: Monday to Friday, 6am–6pm. Closed for refurbishment until early 1995.

KINGSTON

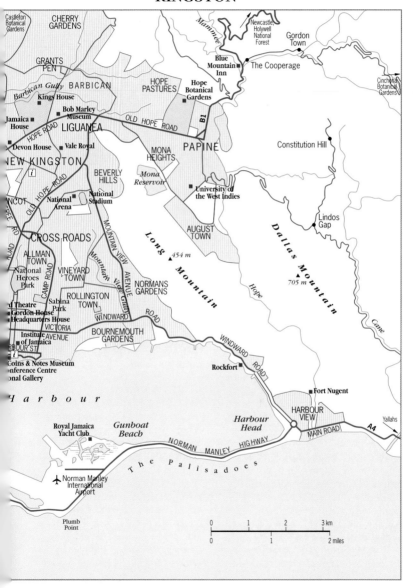

Castleton Botanical Gardens

CHERRY GARDENS

Mammee

Newcastle Holywell National Forest

Gordon Town

GRANTS PEN

Blue Mountain Inn

The Cooperage

Barbican Gully BARBICAN

HOPE PASTURES

Hope Botanical Gardens

Cinchona Botanical Gardens

Kings House

Jamaica House

Bob Marley Museum

OLD HOPE ROAD

LIGUANEA

HOPE ROAD

Devon House

Vale Royal

PAPINE

Constitution Hill

NEW KINGSTON

MONA HEIGHTS

i

BEVERLY HILLS

Mona Reservoir

OLD HOPE ROAD

University of the West Indies

Lindos Gap

NCOT

National Arena

National Stadium

AUGUST TOWN

Long Mountain

Dallas Mountain

CROSS ROADS

454 m

705 m

Hope

ALLMAN TOWN

National Heroes Park

VINEYARD TOWN

NORMANS GARDENS

MOUNTAIN VIEW AVENUE

Mountain View Grant

ROLLINGTON TOWN

Sabina Park

WINDWARD ROAD

Cane

d Theatre

Gordon House

Headquarters House

VICTORIA

BOURNEMOUTH GARDENS

Institute of Jamaica

AVENUE

WINDWARD ROAD

BOUR ST

i

Coins & Notes Museum

onference Centre

onal Gallery

Rockfort

Fort Nugent

Harbour

Harbour Head

HARBOUR VIEW

Yallahs

Royal Jamaica Yacht Club

Gunboat Beach

NORMAN MANLEY HIGHWAY

MAIN ROAD

A4

Norman Manley International Airport

The Palisadoes

Plumb Point

| 0 | 1 | 2 | 3 km |

| 0 | 1 | 2 miles |

The palm trees in front of Devon House are matched by painted ones in the hall

DEVON HOUSE

This stately Georgian mansion was built in 1881 as the residence of George Stiebel, the first black Jamaican millionaire. The handsome structure was constructed entirely by Jamaicans and is set in shady grounds.

The government rescued Devon House from decay in the 1960s to house Jamaica's National Gallery, which has since moved to a new location. It was restored and reopened for a visit by Queen Elizabeth II in January 1983. It is now a museum.

The inside is furnished in 1860s European-colonial style with bewitching hints of the tropics. The entrance hall, for example, has walls decorated with painted palm trees swaying in the breeze. An erstwhile gambling room is discreetly tucked away in the attic.

The old servants' quarters now house an array of boutiques, crafts stores, and shops selling things Jamaican, from polished mahogany furniture to fabled Blue Mountain coffee. Two elegant restaurants, The Grogge Shoppe and The Devonshire, occupy the old stables. *26 Hope Road, Kingston 10 (tel: (809) 929–6602). Open: Tuesday to Saturday, 9am–5pm. Closed Sundays and Mondays. Admission charge.*

GORDON HOUSE

Gordon House was built in 1960 to seat Jamaica's House of Representatives. Within (and in its ceremony) it closely resembles the British House of Commons.

The House was named for the National Hero and martyr George William Gordon, a black legislator, lay preacher, and champion of the poor who was hanged by a kangaroo court in reprisal for the Morant Bay Rebellion in 1865. *Corner of Beeston and Duke Streets (tel: (809) 922–0200). Admission by prior arrangement.*

HEADQUARTERS HOUSE

Parliament formerly sat in this elegant brick and plaster town house built in 1750 by wealthy planter Thomas Hibbert in a wager with three other merchants as to who could build the finest house in order to secure the attentions of a beautiful woman. (Posterity does not record whether Hibbert won his bet.)

Between 1814 and 1872 it served as military headquarters for the island and later as Colonial Secretariat and Ministry of Home Affairs. Today it is the headquarters of the Jamaica National Heritage Trust.

79 Duke Street, Kingston 1 (tel: (809) 922–1287).

HALF WAY TREE

This chaotic crossroads at the junction of Hope Road and Constant Spring Road was once the old village center of St Andrew's Parish. A large clock tower (erected in 1913 as a memorial to King Edward VII) occupies the center.

Half Way Tree is supposedly named for the resting place where an inn catered to travelers heading to and from market.

Constant Spring Road leads north, flanked by aqueducts built in the 1770s on the estate that once stood here.

St Andrew's Parish Church

This church dates back to 1692 and was radically altered in the 1870s. Step inside to admire the organ and stained-glass.

HOPE BOTANICAL GARDENS

These public gardens, the largest botanical gardens in the Caribbean, occupy the old Hope Estate established by Major Richard Hope, who came to Jamaica with Cromwell's army in 1655. The gardens were established by the government in 1881 and today cover some 200 acres below the Blue Mountains.

Pathways lead past a lake, a cactus garden, ornamental ponds, an aquarium, greenhouses, flowering trees, and shrubs. There is also a small zoo and a children's amusement park. The gardens were formerly named the Royal Botanical Gardens in 1953 in honor of Queen Elizabeth II's visit. They are being restored after years of neglect.

Old Hope Road, Kingston 10 (tel: (809) 927–1257). Open: daily, 9am–5:30pm. Admission charge to zoo.

INSTITUTE OF JAMAICA

The Institute was founded in 1879 for "the encouragement of literature, science, and art." This headquarters houses the national archives, including the National Library (formerly the West Indian Reference Library, founded in 1894). The astonishing collection of documents recording the island's history and that of the Caribbean is the largest assemblage of West Indian material in the world.

The Institute's Natural History Division is also here, featuring a herbarium among its attractions. The building has rooms and a lecture hall, plus permanent and visiting exhibitions.

12–16 East Street, Kingston 1 (tel: (809) 922–0620); Open: Monday to Thursday, 9am–5pm; Friday, 9am–4pm. Admission free.

JAMAICA HOUSE

This modern building was built in the 1960s as the residence of the prime minister. Today it is used solely as the prime minister's executive office. It stands behind sentried gates, amid expansive lawns with a driveway lined with lilies, gladioli, and palms. Note the faded Picasso-style mural in the corner of the grounds as you walk up Hope Road.

Hope Road, Kingston 6. Not open to the public.

KINGS HOUSE

This building by noted architect Sir Charles Nicholson is the official residence of the governor-general, the queen's representative on the island. The house replaced an earlier structure, Bishop's Lodge, that was destroyed in the 1907 earthquake and was originally the residence of the lord bishop of Jamaica.

Inside are several valuable paintings, including full-length portraits of King George III and Queen Charlotte by Sir Joshua Reynolds. It is surrounded by 200 acres of well-tended lawns and parkland.

In front of the house is a giant banyan tree that, according to local legend, is occupied by duppies (ghosts).

The governor's wife often invites tourists to tea as part of the Jamaica Tourist Board's Meet the People program.

Hope Road, at the corner of East Kings House Road (tel: (809) 927–6424). Open: Monday to Saturday, 9am–5pm. Currently undergoing refurbishment, contact Jamaica Tourist Board for opening details. Admission free.

NATIONAL GALLERY

Opened in 1984, the National Gallery houses an impressive collection of contemporary and historical works by Jamaica's most exciting artists. The permanent collections include noteworthy sculptures by Edna Manley, the talented wife of the nation's second prime minister, plus almost 100 hardwood sculptures by famed local artist Kapo.

An annual national exhibition is mounted every December.

Roy West Building, 12 Ocean Boulevard (tel: (809) 922–1561). Open: Monday to Friday, 10am–5pm. Admission charge.

NATIONAL HEROES PARK

This former racetrack in the heart of downtown Kingston is now a 75-acre park containing memorials to Jamaica's national heroes: Paul Bogle, George William Gordon, Sam Sharpe, and Maroon chief Nanny. Norman Manley and Alexander Bustamante, the founders of modern Jamaican politics, are both buried here, as are former prime minister Sir Donald Sangster, and Marcus Mosiah Garvey, founder of the Universal Negro Improvement Association.

Simon Bolivar, the South American liberator, and General Antoneo Maceo, a Cuban nationalist hero, are also honored with busts. The Jamaica War Memorial honors the nation's fallen.

Formerly George VI Memorial Park, the park was renamed in 1962 following independence.

North end of Duke Street, ½ mile north of The Parade. Admission free.

SIR WILLIAM GRANT PARK

Sir William Grant Park, in the bustling center of town, is the chaotic terminus for Kingston's bus system. It is commonly known as The Parade and

Mural at the University of the West Indies

was once a military parade ground with a public gallows and stocks. Today the park is shaded by trees laid out in 1870. It has a fountain and several statues to various illustrious Jamaicans. A statue of Queen Victoria faces King Street.

The park is named after a labor leader of the 1930s, who used the steps of Coke Chapel (on the eastern side of the park) as his oratory platform. The chapel, the cradle of Methodism in Jamaica, dates from 1790.
The Parade.

UNIVERSITY OF THE WEST INDIES

The attractive 635-acre campus of the University of the West Indies is wedged between the Hope River and the Long Mountains. The main attraction is the simple, cut-stone chapel near the main entrance. The chapel was transported stone by stone from the Gale Valley Estate in Trelawny (its pediment is inscribed "Edward Morant Gale: 1799").

The university was built in 1948 on the ruins of the old Mona sugar estate. Portions of the aqueduct, plus factory buildings and even a waterwheel, can still be seen.

Stunning murals depicting island life grace the outside walls of the Assembly Hall and Caribbean Mass Communication Building.

The university was originally an appendage of London University; today it is independent, with regional campuses in Jamaica, Trinidad, and Barbados.
Off Mona Road, in the Papine area of Kingston.

VALE ROYAL

The official residence of the prime minister is a beautifully restored, gleaming white, colonnaded colonial

The elegant Ward Theatre in Kingston

structure topped by a dovecote-style lookout tower. The old house has been in continuous use since 1694. It was built by a wealthy planter, Simon Taylor, and later used as the residence of the British colonial secretary.
Montrose Road off Lady Musgrave Road. Not open to the public.

WARD THEATRE

The ornate Ward Theatre was built in 1907 on the site of the municipal Theatre Royal and presented to the city in 1911 by Colonel Charles Ward, Custos of Kingston (see **Politics**). Jamaica's vibrant theatrical traditions still thrive within.

The Ward hosts performances by the National Dance Theatre Company and amateur drama groups, as well as the annual pantomime, which opens on Boxing Day (26 December) and usually runs until April. The patois is often dense, but the spontaneous audience reactions and vivid slapstick style make a visit worthwhile.
North Parade, Kingston 1 (tel: (809) 922–0453).

AROUND KINGSTON

BLUE MOUNTAINS

The majestic Blue Mountains that rise northeast of Kingston are stupendously scenic and easily accessible. The mountains are named for the blue haze that settles in the deep valleys and glazes the peaks, which were heaved from the seabed 25 million years ago.

The mountains are 28 miles east to west, 12 miles north to south, and rise precipitiously to reach 7,402 feet at Blue Mountain Peak. Copious rainfall feeds lush epiphytes and bromeliads. Ferns, palms, bamboo, and mahogany cling to the precipitous slopes. Gnarled elfin forest and alpine meadows are found at higher elevations.

Blue Mountains and John Crow National Park (195,527 acres) was recently established to protect the remaining forests, which resound with a variety of bird calls.

Anyone prepared to negotiate the snaking roads can wind from sea level to mountain peak in less than an hour to enter this realm of clouds, greenery, and breathtaking views.

The temperature drops significantly with altitude. Take a sweater.

The Cooperage

The name is literal. The place, 2 miles north of Papine, takes its name from the Irish coopers who constructed wooden barrels for the export of rum. The coopers lived up the hill in Irish Town.

Just before The Cooperage is Blue Mountain Inn, one of the oldest hostelries in Jamaica.

Cinchona Botanical Gardens

Cinchona clings spectacularly to a ridgetop at over 5,000 feet. The magnificent mountaintop views alone make the arduous journey worthwhile.

Cinchona, 3 miles east of Clydesdale, was established in 1868 to produce Assam tea and cinchona trees, which were grown for quinine from the bark to combat malaria. It proved unprofitable, and the plantations gradually died out. Cinchona was tranformed into an English-style botanical garden.

A wide variety of imported trees and plants include rhododendrons and azaleas that blaze brightly in spring. Dazzlingly colorful lilies bloom in summer. The Great House at the top of the garden is fronted by well-tended lawns.

Cinchona is slowly recovering from damage caused by Hurricane Gilbert in 1988.

You will need a sturdy four-wheel-drive vehicle; otherwise hike.

Hollywell Forest Park

Hollywell, 2 miles north of Newcastle *(tel: (809) 924–2612)*, protects a hauntingly beautiful montane cloud forest. It is also a natural bird sanctuary. Bird song fills the mist-shrouded forest, which is dominated by pines. Wild strawberries and ferns are abundant.

The sanctuary has many marked trails. One leads to a promontory overlooking the city.

Though Hurricane Gilbert demolished many trees, Hollywell has been extensively replanted.

Mavis Bank

This small mountain town is built around Jamaica's oldest working coffee factory: the **Mavis Bank Coffee Factory** (JABLUM), owned by Keble Munn, former Minister of Agriculture. The pulpery is supplied by small-scale

Mountains as far as the eye can see: the view from the hill town of Mavis Bank

coffee producers scattered throughout the mountains. Factory tours are available by appointment *(tel: (809) 924–9503)*. See also page 45.

Newcastle

Newcastle is a Jamaica Defence Force training camp where tourists have access. The cantonment clambers up the hillside from 3,500 to 4,500 feet. The parade ground, bisected by the main road, has a cannon, plus the insignia of Jamaica regiments on the wall. It offers fantastic views down the mountainside to Kingston. With luck, you may be able to time your arrival for a military parade.

The land originally belonged to a French planter who fled from Haiti in 1789. In 1841 the land was sold to the government to establish an army hill station. Until that time British soldiers stationed on the plains died in large numbers from yellow fever. The rows of white tombstones in the military graveyard glow ghostly white in the mists.

A trail marked Woodcutters Gap leads from the road above the camp through an area of wild ginger lilies, tree ferns, and lush forest.

The Blue Mountains rise immediately north of Kingston and extend 25 miles eastward. There is no tourist office. The Forestry Department can provide information (tel: (809) 924-2667).

The amazing Pride of Burma is just one of the blooms at Castleton Botanical Gardens

CASTLETON BOTANICAL GARDENS

Follow the winding A3 north 20 miles from Kingston to reach this fascinating showcase of 1,000 species of native and exotic plants high in the mountains. The 15-acre garden slopes down to the Wag Water River and is well watered by heavy rain.

The gardens were established in 1862 and quickly grew to become the most richly stocked in the Caribbean.

Though Hurricane Gilbert battered this lush Eden severely, the huge tree ferns, azaleas, thirty-five species of palms, and local plants such as *strychnos* (from which strychnine poison is derived) are worth viewing. The densest exhibits are on the left side of the road.
Open: daily, 9am–5pm. Admission free, but guides expect tips.

PORT ROYAL

Relics of Jamaica's most colorful past come alive in Port Royal, the old pirate capital at the tip of the Palisadoes Peninsula, south of Kingston.

The English built a fort here in 1656. Encouraged by the government, buccaneers made the settlement their base for strikes against Spanish ports and ships. Port Royal was soon awash with ale houses and whores – a Babylon of debauchery with the sobriquet "wickedest city in the world." It seemed like a divine judgement when on 7 June 1692 an earthquake and tidal wave toppled two-thirds of it into the harbor.

Though rebuilt and maintained by the British Navy as their West Indian headquarters throughout the 18th century, the town never regained its stature.

Today it is a ramshackle fishing village that still awaits a long-touted restoration. *Attractions are open Monday to Friday, 9am–4pm; weekends, 10am–5pm. A ferry leaves Pier 2 on the Kingston waterfront 7 times daily, 6am–6:30pm; Sunday, 11:20am–6:30pm. No local tourist office.*

Fort Charles

Most impressive of Port Royal's attractions is this landlocked, red-brick fort that was originally surrounded by water. Many of the 104 cannons that pointed to sea in its heyday can still be seen in their embrasures.

British naval hero Horatio Nelson (1758–1805) served as commander here when he was only 20 years old. You can tread in his footsteps on the wooden quarterdeck, warily watching for a French invasion fleet. A plaque tells visitors to "remember his glory."

In the center is a small **Maritime Museum** *(tel: (809) 925–0355)*

containing ship models and intriguing nautical paraphernalia.
Admission charge.

Giddy House

On the foreshore in front of the fort is the old Royal Artillery store up-ended by the earthquake of 1907. It leans at an angle that mildly disorients those stepping inside. Nearby is a huge gun emplacement with a massive cannon lying impotent to the side.

Lime Cay

Some dozen coral cays lie offshore south of Harbour Head spit. Fringed by snow-white sand and shallow turquoise waters, these tiny, uninhabited islets are perfect for snorkeling and sunbathing. Lime Cay is popular with Kingstonians, who picnic here at weekends. Nude bathing is common. The Morgan's Harbour Hotel offers transportation.

Old Naval Hospital

This is a long stone-and-cast-iron building facing the harbor mouth. It dates from 1819. Earthquakes have since reduced it to a state of delapidation. Outside are several equally decrepit horse-drawn carriages.

The building houses the **Archaeological and Historical Museum** *(tel: (809) 924–8706)*, displaying centuries-old relics recovered from the submerged city, which lies just offshore. Among them is a pocket watch with its hands frozen at the moment the earthquake struck.

St Peter's Church

This rather drab building, erected in 1725, is intriguing for the stranger-than-fiction tale of Lewis Galdye Esq, whose gravestone you may spy in the church entrance. The aged slab tells how Galdye "was swallowed up in the Great Earthquake in the Year 1692 & By the Providence of God was by another Shock thrown into the Sea & Miraculously saved by swimming until a Boat took him up." Note the silver plate said to have been taken from the sack of Panama City by Henry Morgan.

Port Royal Maritime Museum

Kingston Walk

Far from the ghettos of downtown Kingston, Uptown (New Kingston) is a relatively prosperous and peaceful residential and business section with several of the city's most appealing architectural gems. Most tourist hotels are a few minutes walk or drive from the starting point. *Allow 2 hours, excluding a museum visit.*

Start at the Jamaica Tourist Board headquarters in the ICWI Building, 2 St Lucia Avenue. Follow Barbados Avenue to Knutsford Boulevard. Turn right and walk three blocks to Trafalgar Road. Turn left and continue to Hope Road. The grounds of Devon House command the northeast corner (note the intriguing, rundown colonial-era structure on the southwest corner that is now the YMCA).

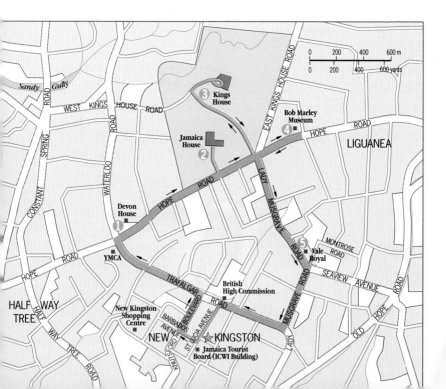

Mural at the Tuff Gong recording studio, now part of the Bob Marley Museum

1 DEVON HOUSE

This elegant mansion, built in 1881, is superbly furnished with period antiques. Behind the house is a fascinating array of boutiques, craft shops, and stores selling everything from ice cream to antique reproductions. The Grogge Shoppe and The Devonshire restaurants are in the former stables and carriage house, where you can dine afresco in the airy courtyard beneath a massive mahogany tree. (See also page 30.)

Continue up Hope Road to Jamaica House.

2 JAMAICA HOUSE

The former residence of the prime minister, with a white-columned portico facing the road, was built in the 1960s. It is fronted by pleasing lawns. (See also page 31.)

Continue along Hope Road to East Kings House Road.

3 KINGS HOUSE

The official residence of the governor-general is set in 200 acres of landscaped grounds. The governor's wife hosts Meet the People tea-parties. Inquire at the Jamaica Tourist Board. (See also page 32.)

Continue up Hope Road to the Bob Marley Museum.

4 BOB MARLEY MUSEUM

The reggae legend's former home and recording studio has been turned into a museum-cum-shrine. The guided one-hour tour offers a fascinating insight into the life of the musical prodigy. In the grounds is the Queen of Sheba restaurant, which serves juices and I-tal vegetarian dishes. (See also page 27.)

Return to East Kings House Road. Turn left onto Lady Musgrave Road. Walk south to the junction of Montrose Road and Seaview Avenue. Turn left. Vale Royal faces you on a right-angle bend.

5 VALE ROYAL

Vale Royal is the residence of the prime minister. The gleaming, two-story wooden structure was built in 1694 by a wealthy planter, Simon Taylor, and later served as the home of the British Colonial Secretary. (See also page 33.)

Return to Lady Musgrave Road and follow it south to Trafalgar Road. Turn right and walk back to St Lucia Avenue. The British High Commission is at the junction.

Port Royal Walk

This straightforward walk takes in the major historic sites – albeit now sadly delapidated – that reflect Port Royal's glory years as the most important city in the Caribbean. You will also get to see something of the local lifestyle that lends Port Royal a funky charm. *Allow 1½ hours.*

Begin at Morgan's Harbour Hotel and Marina. Exit the hotel, turn right, and follow the old dockyard wall to Cagway Road. At the end, cross the public square. Turn left on High Street and follow it to Fisherman's Beach, where pirogues and nets festoon the sand.

Turn left up Broad Street. The Old Naval Hospital is on the right.

1 OLD NAVAL HOSPITAL

The Royal Navy Hospital, built of prefabricated cast-iron segments, has withstood both earthquakes and hurricanes, though it has clearly seen better days. One room houses a basic archaeological museum.

Walk down New Street to Gaol Alley. Turn right.

2 OLD GAOL

The sturdy stone gaol, which predates the 1692 earthquake, has been restored and now houses craft and art stores.

Turn left at the junction of Gaol Alley and Cannon Street. Turn right on Cagway Road and right on Tower Street. Note the parapeted town wall and Half Moon Battery on your left. Continue past St Peter's Church and the Garrison Arch to Nelson Square.

3 NELSON SQUARE

The old parade ground is lined with

barrack buildings, many of which reflect the damage done in 1988 by Hurricane Gilbert.

4 FORT CHARLES
The solid, well-preserved red-brick fort is replete with cannons. A maritime museum is housed in one of the restored buildings in the fort's courtyard.

Exit the fort at its southwest corner and follow the trail to Giddy House and the Victoria and Albert Batteries.

5 GIDDY HOUSE
This lopsided building keeled over during the 1907 earthquake. It once was the Royal Artillery store. Behind is a line of gun batteries, still with massive cannons intact.

Return to Morgan's Harbour Hotel and Marina.

Appropriately named Giddy House

Port Royal, at the end of the Palisadoes Peninsula, is a good day trip from Kingston

Blue Mountains Hike

For the hardy and adventurous nature lover few experiences in Jamaica can top the hike to Blue Mountain Peak (7,402 feet). It is moderately strenuous and usually accomplished in the very early morning hours while still dark. The sunrise, the views as the whole of Jamaica appears in the morning light, and the flora and fauna make for a sublime experience.

Trails from Mavis Bank and Hagley Gap (both reachable by car) lead to Penlyn Castle and then to Whitfield Hall and Abbey Green, where the Blue Mountain Peak trail starts. It is 3,400 feet and 5.8 miles from Abbey Green to the summit. Abbey Green can also be reached by jeep via Hagley Gap, the closest village to the peak.

Plan on overnighting at Whitfield Hall and setting off for the summit before 4am to avoid the clouds that set in by mid-morning. A guide is recommended. *Allow 7 to 8 hours for the round trip from Whitfield Hall.*

From Hagley Gap
Follow the dirt road that leads left from the village square towards Penlyn Castle. Bearing right, continue past Whitfield Hall to Abbey Green (4.2 miles).

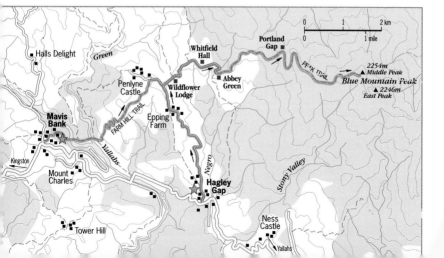

From Mavis Bank

Follow the steep, narrow footpath to Penlyn Castle (5.5 miles). A local can point the way. From there, leave the Post Office (on your right) and follow the road past Wildflower Lodge and Whitfield Hall to Abbey Green (1.7 miles).

The path to the summit is clearly marked, though lined with thick foliage. It switchbacks steeply through fountain-like glades of bamboo and ferns. Above 5,500 feet are stunted, gnarled trees – a rare remnant of cloud forest – festooned with mosses and epiphytes. The only sounds are chirrups and peepings of insects and frogs. The only lights are the phosphorescence of fireflies and occasional views of Kingston twinkling like a galaxy far below.

Windswept scrub commands the flat-topped summit, where there is a small hut. It will be chilly, with a strong wind.

The sunrise alone is worth the hike. As the sun crests the horizon, ridge after mountain ridge emerges; then the whole island receding into the blue mist. On a clear day Cuba can be seen riding the northern horizon.

Do not dally at the top. There is much to admire as you descend: colorful birds and butterflies, dwarf orchids, honeysuckle, rhododendrons, and the pendulous blossoms of "Jamaican rose" (merianias) that seem to glow from within when struck by sunlight.

Accommodations

Four guest houses/hostels between Penlyn and Abbey Green provide basic dormitory accommodations and kitchen facilities:

Wildflower Lodge: Beds, cooking, water, meals prepared on request *(tel: (809) 926-5874)*.

Whitfield Hall: Beds, cooking, water, meals prepared on request *(tel: (809) 927-0986)*.

Abbey Green: Beds, cooking, camping *(tel: (809) 922-8705)*.

Maya Lodge: Rooms, camping, guides *(Jack's Hill; tel: (809) 927-2097)*.

The Forestry Department maintains a shelter at Portland Gap (2.3 miles beyond Abbey Green). Bring your own bedding. Water is usually available.

Welcome sight en route from Mavis Bank

When to go

December to April and June to September provide the best hiking weather. However, rain can fall on any day of the year and the weather can change hour by hour. May, and late September to November, are the rainiest months.

What to take

It can be cool by day and cold at night, conditions which are exacerbated by dampness and wind. Dress warmly. Bring a sweater and/or jacket, plus raingear. The terrain is rugged and slippery in places; wear sturdy shoes or boots. Take fruit, nuts, and/or other energy food, plus bottled water. A flashlight is essential.

Blue Mountains Drive

Off this circle are trails, forest preserves, interesting houses, coffee plantations, and gardens. The roads are deeply potholed (a Jeep is preferable), but the fabulous views make amends. There are few signposts; check your directions with locals. An early start is essential to avoid the mid-morning clouds that settle over the Blue Mountains. Drive with care; the narrow roads hug the mountains. Use your horn on bends. *Allow 5–6 hours, including stops.*

Start at Half-Way Tree. Follow Hope Road past Devon House, Bob

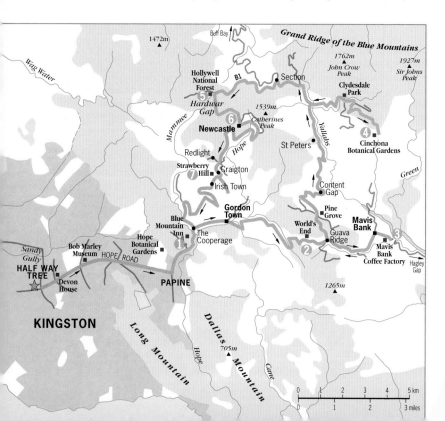

*Marley Museum, and Hope Botanical
Garden. Keep left at Papine. After about 6
miles, the Blue Mountain Inn is on the left.*

1 BLUE MOUNTAIN INN
Originally a coffee plantation house, the
Blue Mountain Inn is now one of
Jamaica's finest restaurants. The
atmosphere has changed little over the
centuries. Jackets are required for men
(tel: (809) 927–1700).

*Continue uphill to Gordon Town, named
after the Gordon Highlanders, who were
billeted nearby. Turn right over the narrow
bridge. The road winds steeply uphill, with
sweeping views over Kingston. After 5 miles,
World's End is on your left, with a mural
painted on the outside wall.*

2 WORLD'S END
This mountainside factory produces
Sangster's "Old Jamaica" liqueurs and
rums. There are fine views towards
Newcastle from the outside patio. Call
ahead for a tour *(tel: (809) 926–8888).*

*Continue one mile to Guava Ridge; then
straight to Mavis Bank (3 miles).*

3 MAVIS BANK COFFEE FACTORY
Jamaica's oldest coffee factory
(JABLUM). A factory tour is available.
Call ahead *(tel: (809) 924-9503).*

*Return to Guava Ridge. Turn right at the
sign for Pine Grove. Beyond St Peters (5
miles) is a junction for Clydesdale. Turn
right; it is a rough drive or a 2-hour hike to
Cinchona.*

4 CINCHONA BOTANICAL GARDENS
Founded in 1868 to grow cinchona trees,
whose bark produces quinine to combat
malaria, the gardens cling to a
mountaintop ridge. Rhododendrons and
azaleas are seen at their best in spring,
while lilies bloom in abundance in early
summer.

*Return via Clydesdale to the junction. Turn
right for Section, where the road joins the
B1. Bear left for Hardwar Gap. After about
3 miles the entrance to Hollywell National
Forest is on the right.*

5 HOLLYWELL FOREST PARK
Part of Blue Mountains and John Crow
National Park, Hollywell has one of the
few remaining montane forests in
Jamaica. There are lovely picnic spots
and trails.

Follow the B1 south to Newcastle.

6 NEWCASTLE
This military camp, established in 1841,
nestles idyllically on the mountainside.
The parade ground, replete with cannon
and regimental insignia, offers a
spectacular view over Kingston.

*The road drops steeply past Craigton Estate.
Below Redlight, follow the sign right up a
steep, forbidding road to Strawberry Hill.*

7 STRAWBERRY HILL
This restored 17th-century Great House
is now a luxurious plantation-style hotel
and restaurant where guests can enjoy a
good 360-degree view *(tel: (809)
944–8235).*

*Continue downhill through Irish Town,
named after the Irish coopers who
constructed the barrels in which rum was
exported in the 19th century. Turn right at
The Cooperage for Kingston.*

BLUE MOUNTAIN COFFEE

America. Coffee cognoscenti regard Blue Mountain coffee with something akin to adoration – novelist Ian Fleming, who lived part-time in Jamaica, would not let his literary hero James Bond drink any other.

Coffee has been grown in the Blue Mountains since 1728, when the Jamaican governor, Sir Nicholas Lawes, imported seedlings from Martinique. Cultivation spread quickly. The boom quickened following the revolution in Haiti in 1790, when many skilled coffee growers fled to Jamaica. By 1840 coffee exports had risen to 17,000 tons a year.

With the final abolition of slavery in 1838, decline set in. By 1951, when a hurricane sheared most of the plants off the mountains, the industry was almost dead.

Jamaica's Blue Mountains are a promised land for the coffee tree, which here produces beans of world-famed quality. The angle and aspect of the well-drained slopes, together with the subtle combinations of minerals, sunshine, and cool mountain mists, conspire to produce a healthy berry that gives a full-bodied, aromatic coffee with an exceptionally fine, earthy flavor.

Jamaica's coffee comes from the arabica bean, which is far more flavorful than the robusta bean grown in South

In 1973, the Jamaican government established the Coffee Industry Board to stimulate the dying industry. Strict quality controls were enacted, and the government regulated the Blue Mountain coffee name.

Today, about 28,000 acres are devoted to coffee cultivation, but only 9,000 are legally within the bounds of the Blue Mountain parameters: above 2,000 feet. The richest, mildest coffee grows near the plant's uppermost

Various stages in the production of delicious
Blue Mountain Coffee

The hand-picked berries are trucked or
carried by donkey to the pulperies, where they are
scrubbed, washed, dried, and then sorted
according to size and shape before being sold to
the Coffee Industry Board or roasted (often over a
smoky wood fire) and vacuum-sealed to retain the
fragrance characteristic of Blue Mountain Coffee.
Almost the entire crop is exported to Japan,
where Blue Mountain Coffee
is a status symbol and
pampered palates are
prepared to pay up to $15 a
cup (many of the few large
plantations that exist are
owned by Japanese
companies, which invested
heavily in the Jamaican coffee
industry in the early 1980s).

altitudinal limits, where the bean takes
longer to matu   Other coffee beans are
known as High Mountain Blend, or
Lowland, depending on their origin.
    The pulperies (processing plants)
are supplied by more than 4,000 small
and medium-sized farms scattered
throughout the mountains. In April, with
the first rains, small white blossoms
burst forth and the air is laced with
jasmine-like perfume. By November the
glossy, 2m-tall bushes are plump with
shiny red berries.

The East

*J*amaica's far east should be flush with tourists. It is not, though it was the island's first resort region and has a long history of celebrity patronage. The rich and famous still relax here—understandably, for it is easy to fall in love with the windward coast's slow pace and rugged scenery. Resolutely old-fashioned with its easy charm, Port Antonio has some of Jamaica's most up-scale hotels.

A sense of near-perfect inaccessibility protects this staggeringly beautiful corner from mass tourism—that, and the rains. The area receives three times as much rain as Montego Bay and Ocho Rios (to be fair, it generally falls at night).

Hurricane Gilbert swept through in September 1988, destroying vegetation and roads. The roads remain damaged, but the rains have restored everything else to its former glory. Giant ferns and bamboo brush against your car, and the hills that rise towards the serried John Crow and cloud-covered Blue Mountains are buried under tumbles of plumbagos, morning glory, and

EAST JAMAICA

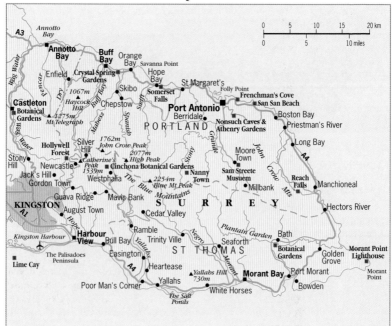

Just one of the views from the aptly named Bonnie View Hotel, Port Antonio. Informal and relaxed, the town is less commercialized than the big resort towns on the north coast

poinsettias, red as bright lipstick and blue as the fabulously clear sky high up above.

No coral reef protects this windward shore. The road rises, dips, and curves past wave-chewed rocky headlands. Deep bays beckon surfers – Boston and Long Bays are the finest. Lonely fishing villages are tucked in the coves. The south-facing shores are more sheltered and lined with beautiful, expansive beaches east of Morant.

Diversions are many in the eastern part of the island. In the 1960s rafting the Rio Grande by moonlight was considered the quintessence of romance, until a formally dressed party tipped unceremoniously over into the water. However you can still find amusement rafting Jamaica's longest river by day.

Reach Falls and Somerset Falls provide refreshing distractions, as do Nonsuch Caves (pretty and generally free of tourist buses). Crystal Springs, a quasibotanical garden, has several nature attractions. Off-the-beaten-path Bath, surrounded by fields of sugarcane as green as ripe limes, also has a botanical garden, plus piping-hot mineral springs.

Game fishing is another prime attraction – if the lure strikes, head out into the indigo ocean to hunt a blue marlin in the island's finest fishing grounds.

Alternatively, you may wish simply to settle in quaint Port Antonio or one of the nearby private coves and while away your days contemplating the mysterious and welcome lack of tourists in this little known corner of the island.

Port Antonio

*M*ovie hero Errol Flynn, who settled here when his yacht washed ashore, described Port Antonio as "more beautiful than any woman I've ever seen." Latter-day tourists may be surprised at this. A first pass through this sleepy, melancholic backwater can invoke a numb we've-made-a-terrible-mistake expression.

Persevere and you will soon understand why Port Antonio, a 2-hour drive from Kingston or Ocho Rios, still attracts royalty and movie stars.

During the late 19th century Port Antonio was a bustling banana port. Around 1890 Captain Lorenzo Dow Baker, founder of the Boston Fruit Company, began bringing tourists from cold New York City in his empty banana boats. Hotels sprouted and Port Antonio was launched as the first tourist resort in

Jamaica. A Who's Who of unwinding internationals adopted the town, such as financier J P Morgan, movie star Bette Davis, author Rudyard Kipling, and, later, Errol Flynn.

The wild parties that Flynn hosted here are no more. The cruise ships long ago decamped to livelier Ocho Rios. And though they still load bananas down at Boundbrook Wharf, that candle too barely flickers.

Boundbrook Wharf, Port Antonio: quiet now that the film stars have sailed away

PORT ANTONIO

Today Port Antonio, 67 miles east of Ocho Rios, is a rakish, rundown maritime harbor. The genteel lifestyle lingers on, however, at sumptuous hotels – most of which are hidden in their own secret coves – where the waiters still call female guests "m'lady."

It takes no more than 2 hours to walk and see Port Antonio. The town nestles between two scenic harbors with garbage-strewn beaches. A good way to get your bearings is from atop the hill south of town.

A walk down the 2 main streets – Harbour and West Streets – will give you a sense of provincial Jamaican life; make sure to drop in at Musgrave Market, a great place to buy craft work. Tread carefully or you will disturb the goats that snooze beneath the clock tower in front of the Courthouse.

Before exploring farther afield peek in Christ Church, a prim, red-brick edifice

that dominates Port Antonio; then visit Navy Island, the former hideaway once owned by Errol Flynn. Alas, the town's Victorian-style gingerbread houses are woebegone, but De Montevin Lodge begs a visit.

Port Antonio is a popular movie set – it is supposed to have featured in more films than anywhere else in the Caribbean, among them *Lord of the Flies*, *Mighty Quinn*, *Club Paradise*, and *Cocktail*.

The town's greatest assets are the tiny, talc-textured beaches east of the town and the game fish that swim not too far out to sea (the prestigious Port Antonio Blue Marlin Tournament is held each October). Oh, yes, and the lack of tourism is precisely what makes Port Antonio so appealing.

The Jamaica Tourist Board office (tel: (809) 993–3051) is located upstairs at City Centre Shopping Plaza, on Harbour Street.

The clear waters of the Blue Lagoon are ideal for a quick dip

Blue Lagoon

The Blue Lagoon is a 180-feet-deep cup in the coast, actually a limestone sinkhole filled with deep azure waters. The beautiful spot, 5 miles east of Port Antonio, is surrounded by deep-green jungle. It is fed by freshwater springs that seep up into the saltwater lagoon.

The lagoon, locally called "Blue Hole," is good for swimming and snorkeling. Locals take glee in telling you, incorrectly, that Errol Flynn dived to the bottom. By day you may take a glass-bottomed boat ride; the translucent waters are floodlit at night.

Yes, the movie *Blue Lagoon* was filmed here. *Club Paradise* was also filmed here – alas, the waterfront restaurant was demolished by Hurricane Gilbert in 1988. The hawkers are persistent; escape by diving into the pellucid waters.

Bonnie View

Drive up Richmond Hill to this venerable landmark hotel for the view. The property (built in 1943) is perched on a promontory that offers a splendid 360-degree view over the town, coast, and Blue Mountains. The 25 acres of carefully cultivated grounds are good for horseback riding and a plantation tour.

Boundbrook Wharf

Boundbrook Wharf, on West Harbour, was once the main deep-water pier of the United Fruit Company. It was the inspiration for Harry Belafonte's "Banana Boat Song."

Today there are no stevedores "working all night on a drink of rum" or waiting for the tallyman to tally their bananas. But you can still see bananas being loaded on to boats bound for Europe and North America.

Christ Church

This neo-Romanesque, red-brick Anglican church at the east end of Harbour Street was built in 1840. It is impressive within and has a brass lectern that was donated by the Boston Fruit Company in 1900.
West Palm Avenue and Harbour Street.

De Montevin Lodge

You do not need to stay at De Montevin Lodge to appreciate its homey beauty. The red-brick, gingerbread-trimmed guest house boasts carved hardwood doorways and staircase, impressive colored tilework, Tiffany lamps, and chintz sofas that will remind you of grandma's old parlor.

The structure was built as a town house by the Hon. David Gideon, Custos of Portland Parish (see **Politics**) at the turn of the century.
Titchfield Street.

Fort George

Fort George dates from 1729. In its heyday it was one of the most powerful forts in the Caribbean. It stands on the peninsula that divides East and West Harbour.

Since 1875 it has been occupied by the Titchfield High School, whose

Fort George, Port Antonio, now a school

playground was once the military parade ground. The tip of the promontory, behind the school, was the bastion – you can still see embrasures for twenty-two cannons in its 10-foot-thick walls. A few of the cannons remain.

Bananas are still shipped from Boundbrook Wharf to Europe and North America

The enticing golden sands and azure sea of secluded Frenchman's Cove

Folly

Follow the headland east of East Harbour and you will reach a pseudo-Grecian estate lying roofless under the sun. The shell is that of a sixty-room mansion built in 1905 by an American millionaire, Alfred Mitchell, for his lady love, a Tiffany heiress. Alas, says local legend, he used sea water in the cement, causing the structure to quickly dissolve. Castle and lady both disappeared, leaving only a legendary ruin, appropriately called Folly.

In reality salt air rusted the steel reinforcement rods and the roof caved in. Columns of Jamaican limestone have stood the test of time.

Frenchman's Cove

This cosy little cove, 2 miles east of town, protects a boutique beach where you may bathe topless. A gin-clear stream winds lazily between the lava-rock headlands and spills on to the beach.

In the 1950s a millionaire built what was acclaimed as the most expensive hotel in the world atop the cliffs. For a while, Frenchman's Cove was a place where royalty soaked up the sun. The hotel no longer operates, and you may even have the beach to yourself. *Admission charge.*

Monkey Island

Yes, monkeys once roamed free on this tiny jewel, a short distance off San San Beach. When American millionaire Alfred Mitchell (see *Folly*, above) stocked it with monkeys, it was called Pellew Island. It can be reached by swimming or boating.

Navy Island

This island, just offshore of West Harbour, was once a base for the British Royal Navy. In later years movie star Errol Flynn bought the 60-acre island and used it as a private hideaway to entertain beautiful young starlets. The Admiralty Club, a resort-cum-marina on a nautical theme boasts memorabilia of the movie star *(tel: (809) 993-2667)*.

There are two beaches, one where you may acquire full-body tan.
Take the 7-minute ferry ride from the Navy Island dock on West Street. Water taxis leave every ½ hour, 24 hours a day.

San San Beach

Scintillating talcum-fine sand encusped in parentheses headlands explain the appeal of San San Beach. The half-moon cove, about 5 miles east of Port Antonio, has long been colonized by the wealthy.

Three hotels share the private beach, but nonguests are welcome. The stairway to the beach descends through thick, wild greenery. The beach is backed by a golf course (nine-hole) hacked from the overgrown valley with machetes.

San San Beach, where the rich play

Offshore is Princess Island, which a wealthy socialite – Baron Heinrich Thyssen – gave as a honeymoon gift to his wife.
Open: daily, 9am–5pm. Admission charge.

ERROL FLYNN

In 1947 movie hero Errol Flynn washed up in Jamaica when his yacht Zacca was blown ashore by a storm. Quite taken with the place – "When God created Eden, this is what he was aiming at," he wrote – Flynn bought Navy Island as well as the Titchfield Hotel, a watering hole for the likes of Rudyard Kipling, and even a cattle ranch on Priestman's River.

Flynn swashbuckled his way around Jamaica in typical Hollywood fashion. He organized raft races on the Rio Grande and threw wild parties that are the stuff of local legend. His beguiling ways attracted other Hollywood stars. This select bunch put Port Antonio and Jamaica on the map.

Navy Island, once owned by Errol Flynn

In a way, Flynn never left. His widow Patrice Wymore Flynn is still seen about town or on her ranch, where she raises Red Poll cattle. It is easy to imagine the sun-bronzed screen idol strolling along the beach, hair tousled by the wind and trousers rolled up, on his way for a drink.

The Cathedral, one of the Nonsuch Caves discovered by a goat in 1955

ANNOTTO BAY

Sleepy, ramshackle Annotto Bay straggles along the coast, midway between Ocho Rios and Port Antonio, at the junction of the road across the Blue Mountains to Kingston. An old train station, now disused, once bustled during the banana boom when Annotto handled the produce from forty-eight estates.

Take time to peek inside the slightly baroque-style Baptist Church, near the market square. The yellow-and-red brick structure, built in 1894, has intriguing decorative plaster motifs.

The town is named after an orange dye made from the seeds of the *bixa orellana*, or anatta tree, used by Arawak Indians for body paints.

ATHENRY GARDENS

Sci-fi size heliconia, poinciana, and bird of paradise blossom madly in these neatly tended gardens on a 185-acre coconut plantation high in the hills overlooking Port Antonio. The cafeteria offers refreshing beer and soft drinks; its pavilion provides intoxicating views.
Nonsuch, 2 miles south of Port Antonio (tel: (809) 993-3740). Open: daily, 9am–5pm. Admission charge.

Nonsuch Caves

Complete your visit to Athenry with a peek inside Nonsuch Caves. Well-lit concrete pathways lead through nine chambers formed long before Jamaica rose above the sea – fish and other sea creatures swam through the dark depths, as evidenced by the fossils found there.

Bats hang from the lofty ceiling in the Cathedral, or Bat Romance Room, which accurately describes what goes on. Your guide will conjure up imaginative forms from the coral formations: a bishop, a man in robes upon a camel, even a naked woman emerging from a shell.
3 miles southeast of Port Antonio. Open: daily, 9am–5pm. Admission charge.

BATH

During Victorian days Bath was the most fashionable resort in Jamaica. Today it is rather rundown but worth a visit for two singular attractions. Then, as now, it was surrounded by sugarcane fields and, to the north, by the soaring Blue Mountains from the base of which burble steaming hot springs.

The springs were discovered in 1699 when a slave who had been wounded in seeking his freedom was healed after bathing in the pools. The government appointed the directors of the Bath of St

The Bath Fountain Hotel where you can soak your ailments away – allegedly

Thomas the Apostle to oversee the administration of the baths. Accommodations were built in 1747, and thirty slaves were purchased to maintain the road.
47 miles east of Kingston.

Bath Fountain Hotel
This colonial-style hotel *(tel: (809) 982–2132)*, 2 miles north of town, still has natural hot spring baths open to the casual passerby. A 20-minute soak will supposedly cure "bellyache and venereal disease, all capillary obstructions, and diseases of the breast proceeding from weakness or want of proper glandular secretions . . .

consumption and nervous spasms, not to mention rheumatism and 'depraved appetite'." Whatever, you will emerge feeling like a relaxed, if rather boiled, lobster.

Bath Botanical Gardens
The arboretum and garden, next to Bath's venerable white stone church, were the island's first. Planted in 1779, the gardens have since shrunk in size, though they remain of great charm. Many of Jamaica's imported plants first took root here, including bougainvillea, cinnamon, jacaranda, and the breadfruit brought from the South Seas by Captain William Bligh.

BOSTON BAY
Your first, idyllic, impression of Boston Bay, 9 miles east of Port Antonio, is of a wide crescent of white sand enclosed in a pleasing cove. When calm the water is like a turquoise jewel; when the sea is up massive waves crash ashore, drawing surfers. There are plenty of water sports to choose from.

This is where Jamaica's commercial "jerk" legend began. The well-maintained public beach is rimmed by stalls where chicken, lobster, and wild boar sizzle in pepper-sauce marinade. Jerk was created by the Maroons who hunted boar in the nearby mountains. Wild boar are still hunted, and on any day you can smell it being slow-cooked over pimento wood. You can buy some along with puddles of spicy sauce and piles of fried "festival" dumplings.

LONG BAY

Jamaica's dramatic coastal scenery reaches its zenith at Long Bay, where strong winds push waves forcefully ashore onto two wide, scimitar-shaped beaches backed by palms. The deep turquoise waters are marred by an unpredictable undertow.

Modernist painter Ken Abendana Spencer welcomes visitors interested in Jamaican culture and art to his fortress-like studio home in the hills above town. *14 miles east of Port Antonio. The Spencer Studio is on Lyssons Road (tel: (809) 982-2336). Turn right at the post office (just east of the service station). No regular opening hours. Admission free.*

MANCHIONEAL

Manchioneal is a sleepy fishing village, an away-from-it-all place of peace and quiet set in a deep, scalloped bay with calm turquoise waters and a narrow beach. Fishing pirogues add a dash of color. The hamlet is named after the poisonous seaside plant that used to grow here.

MOORE TOWN

Lonesome Moore Town is the capital of the Windward Maroons (see **Maroons**, page 75). The small village is scattered along a stream course 10 miles south of Port Antonio via a steep, winding dirt road. En route, you may see Maroon descendants carrying bananas in traditional head slings.

The Maroons harassed the British army and plantocracy from their redoubts in the John Crow Mountains for almost a century. In 1734 the British finally flushed the Maroons from their mountain fortress at Nanny Town and five years later signed a peace treaty that established Moore Town as the Maroons' capital.

Moore Town and its environs are a semiautonomous political unit (note the Jamaican and Maroon flags that fly together). A Maroon "Colonel" presides over a committee of twenty-four elected council members. Village meetings take

Cricket is the Jamaican passion: seen here in a rustic setting at Moore Town

place on the common, or recreation ground, known as *Osofu*.

A small museum tells of Maroon history. You will need guides if you plan on exploring farther afield.

Ask the Jamaica Tourist Board (tel: (809) 993–3051) to make arrangements for you to visit and to meet the Maroon Colonel.

Bump Grave

The simple stone monument opposite the school is Bump Grave, where according to legend the remains of Maroon leader Nanny are buried. Nanny was imbued with supernatural powers. It was recorded that she "received the bullets of the enemy that were aimed at her and returned them with fatal effect, in a manner of which decency forbids a nearer description." The government declared her a national heroine in 1975 and erected the memorial.

MORANT BAY

Follow the coast road east from Port Antonio and you will eventually reach the town of Morant Bay, on the southeast coast. In the town square is a statue of Paul Bogle, a Jamaican preacher who was hanged by the British in the aftermath of the 1865 Morant Bay rebellion. The statue is the work of the Honourable Edna Manley, wife and mother of former Jamaican prime ministers.

Bogle had led a protest march during a period of unemployment and poverty when tensions ran high. The authorities fired into the crowd, inciting a riot in which twenty-eight people were killed and the court house burned down. Martial law was declared, thousands of men and women were flogged, and 430 were executed in reprisal for the rioting. A Royal Commission found that the

punishment was "positively barbarous." The British parliament reacted by dissolving the Jamaican House of Assembly, and Jamaica was named a Crown Colony.

Morant Bay Fort, behind the rebuilt Courthouse, dates from 1773. It still has cannons and a park containing the graves of seventy-eight of the victims executed in 1865. The town's red-brick Anglican Christ Church dates from 1881.

The church at Moore Town

MORANT POINT LIGHTHOUSE

A red-and-white-hooped lighthouse marks Morant Point, below Holland Bay, Jamaica's easternmost headland.

The cast-iron edifice, built in 1841, is reached from the tumbledown village of Golden Grove along muddy tracks that meander intestinally through the sugarcane fields of the Tropicana Sugar Estates. Hire a guide!

The lighthouse keeper will gladly show the way 100 feet to the top. It is windy up here, but the powerful view and the silence make for a profound experience.

REACH FALLS

At Manchioneal a newly paved road (a great relief after the pitted main highway) leads inland and climbs through the foothills of the John Crow Mountains to secluded Reach Falls. You are welcomed by Rastas selling tams, necklaces, and carved calabash gourds.

A path leads downhill past a mossy cliff-face to the tumbling river. The falls cascade from one jade-colored pool to another. You may plunge into the effervescent waters but note the sign that warns: "Beware of deep pools and strong currents." A ½-mile hike upriver leads to a whirlpool inside Mandingo Cave.

There are toilets and a bar, and a restaurant that serves fare such as tuna fish stew with potatoes.

You can also investigate the cave that lies behind the Reach Falls

RIO GRANDE

The island's largest river is also its oldest tourist attraction. Local farmers once floated bananas downstream to St Margaret's Bay, 4 miles west of Port Antonio. When movie hero Errol Flynn arrived (see **Errol Flynn**, page 55), he organized raft races and took his friends rafting – it is said that he used to make the trip twice a day, but never with the same woman!

The ride from Berridale to the river mouth, navigating shoals and steep-sided gorges, is still a favorite with tourists. The journey takes about 3 hours. En route, you will glide past rustic villages and some of the loveliest scenery in Jamaica. Riverside vendors, even musicians, serve the river traffic. It is very romantic, especially on full-moon nights.

Trips begin and end at Rafter's Rest, St Margaret's Bay. Rio Grande Attractions

Ltd, P O Box 128, Port Antonio (tel: (809) 993-2778).

SOMERSET FALLS

This pleasing picnic and hiking spot 1 mile east of Hope Bay is set in a cool, shady canopy where the Daniels River cascades through lush forest. A raftsman will pole you gondola-like to the base of the falls, where you may plunge Tarzan-like from a high rock. Ginger lilies, heliconia, and wild bananas grow profusely.

There are restrooms and a small jerk restaurant. Silver perch are raised in an adjacent fish farm, fed by water from the falls.

Open: daily, 9am–5pm. Admission charge.

STOKES HALL

Two miles south of Golden Grove you will see Stokes Hall to the east, sitting atop a hill. The impressive, albeit overgrown remains are those of a fortified Great House dating back to the 17th century and built by one of the three sons of Governor of Jamaica Luke Stokes, who died of swamp fever in 1660.

A farmer stands in front of the ruins of 17th-century Stokes Hall

1780–1, "he fought, often singlehandedly, a war of terror against the English soldiers and planters who held the slave territory. Strong, brave, skilled with machete and musket, his bold exploits were equalled only by his chivalry." He was ambushed and killed in 1781.

YALLAHS

Cattle wander through the street of ramshackle Yallahs. The village, 20 miles east of Kingston, sits amid arid scrubland and is in itself of no particular interest. The wide and usually dry Yallahs River, west of town, washes great swathes of boulders and pebbles over the road during flash storms.

Kach Mansong Memorial

On the hillside 6 miles west of Yallahs is a roadside marker placed by the Jamaican National Heritage Trust in honor of Kach Mansong, or "Three-finger Jack."

The tablet tells us that in these hills, in

Salt Ponds

On the eastern outskirts of Yallahs you will pass by two huge, shallow lakes of soupy water separated from the sea by a narrow spit. These incredibly briny ponds teem with brine shrimp and micro-organisms that attract wading birds. They are occasionally used to extract salt and in the 18th century produced 10,000 bushels of salt annually.

The ponds often flare bright red. Though legend claims it is the blood of slaves murdered here, it is actually caused by bacteria that bloom during drought, emitting a powerful stench.

Port Antonio Walk

A run-down banana port of tropical languor, Port Antonio nonetheless offers a handful of intriguing attractions and two particularly appealing vistas best enjoyed on a walking tour. *Allow 1½ hours, or 2½ hours including Bonnie View.*

Start at the Jamaica Tourist Board upstairs at City Plaza on Harbour Street. You can park across the road in front of the Courthouse.

1 COURTHOUSE AND CLOCK TOWER

This handsome red-brick Georgian building is adorned with a cupola and iron verandas. It dominates the town square, which features a clock tower.

Cross Harbour Street at the square's southeast corner and enter the lively Musgrave Market for a quick browse. Return to the square and turn left on Fort George Street. Walk uphill 150 yards.

2 DeMONTEVIN LODGE

This venerable hotel, the former home of an English sea captain, still has mahogany furniture, gingerbread highlights, and charm aplenty. Even if you do not stay here, come for lunch or dinner – the Jamaican food is excellent *(tel: (809) 993–2604)*.

Continue along Fort George Street to the end of the peninsula. En route you will pass several quaint houses, some decorated with gingerbread fretwork relics of the town's heyday.

3 TITCHFIELD SCHOOL (FORT GEORGE)

It is difficult to tell where Titchfield School ends and Fort George begins. Parts of the fortifications still stand (the main school building was the old barracks), along with several cannons.

Turn right from Fort George Street and follow Gideon Avenue back into town. The view across the bay towards the Blue Mountains begs a camera. Follow the waterfront to the Jamaica Arcade craft market, on the right. After a brief stop, continue to Harbour Street. Turn right. Turn left onto West Palm Avenue.

4 PARISH CHURCH OF PORTLAND

The red-brick Anglican church was built in neo-Romanesque style and completed in 1840. The brass lectern was presented in 1900 by the Boston Fruit Company.

Continue along West Palm Avenue to the five-way junction (note the pretty green-and-ochre wooden building on the left).

Left: the town square's clock tower

A delicate wrought-iron balcony adorns the front of DeMontevin Lodge Hotel

Turn right on to William Street and walk to West Street. Note the cenotaph at the junction. Turn right and return to the main square.
Alternatively, if energetic, follow the sign for Bonnie View at the five-way junction. The road switchbacks steeply for half a mile to the Bonnie View Hotel.

5 BONNIE VIEW HOTEL

This pleasing hotel has an airy veranda where you can savor one of the best coastal views in Jamaica while cooling off with an iced drink. Refuel here, too, with a hearty, moderately priced lunch, or linger for sunset *(tel: (809) 993–2752)*.

The hotel will drive you back down to town in their van.

Port Antonio Drive

This drive reveals the "other side of Jamaica," whose Manchioneal District has been designated by the UN as one of the world's pristine wilderness areas. The road squiggles along a coastline hammered by waves, past sandy coves and through a riotous rain forest that hides dazzling waterfalls. *Allow 5 hours, including stops.*

Leave Port Antonio on the A4 heading east. In about 5 miles, San San Beach and Blue Hole are on the left.

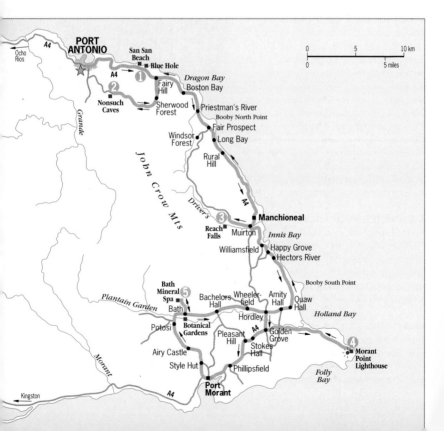

1 SAN SAN BEACH AND BLUE HOLE

A supremely pretty beach backed by several luxurious villas. Good snorkeling on the reef. Monkey Island beckons offshore. Immediately south is Blue Hole, a 180-foot-deep seawater lagoon of deepest azure fed by springs said to have rejuvenating powers on the libido.

Go ½ mile east, turn right at Fairy Hill for Nonsuch Caves.

2 NONSUCH CAVES

Nine deep limestone chambers are adorned with stalactites, stalagmites, and fossilized sponges. The lighted caves are traversed by concrete walkways. Bats flit overhead.

Return to Fairy Hill and continue east, passing a series of beautiful bays lined with white-sand beaches. Boston Bay is supposedly where jerk pork was invented. On the left are the Errol Flynn Estates, still run by his widow Patrice Wymore. The John Crow Mountains loom to the right. Half a mile beyond Manchioneal turn right for Reach Falls.

3 REACH FALLS

The crystal waters of the Driver's River cascade over escarpments. A dip in the cool, effervescent waters is a refreshing experience.

Return to the A4. Continue south past Hectors River, where the road cuts inland through the Tropicana Sugar Estates. Turn left at the crossroads at Hordley. One mile farther is Golden Grove. Gluttons for bad roads might turn left at the gasoline station after hiring a guide to escort them through the sugarcane fields to Morant Point Lighthouse.

The Morant Point Lighthouse

4 MORANT POINT LIGHTHOUSE

This lonesome, 100-foot-tall, cast-iron lighthouse – a National Historic Landmark – was fashioned in London in 1841. The keeper will guide you to the top for fabulous views across the plains to the Blue Mountains.

Return to Golden Grove. Turn left for Port Morant. From here a road to the right winds uphill to Bath. Turn left opposite the Botanical Gardens and follow the winding road for a mile and a half.

5 BATH MINERAL SPA

A once-popular, now somewhat rundown spa resort that still offers private mineral baths that promise a cure for many ills *(tel: (809) 982–2132)*. Stroll the botanical garden.

Continue east 6 miles to Hordley along a badly potholed road. Return to Port Antonio.

The North Coast

*J*amaica's lush north coast is a fusion of green hills and sculptured sand crescents – an idyllic setting for two of the island's prime tourist resorts, Ocho Rios and Runaway Bay. Many of Jamaica's premier sightseeing attractions and natural wonders are concentrated along the north coast between Falmouth and Port Maria.

Farther east the magnificent seascapes build toward a crescendo. The sea, the color of melted peridots, opens up fully. The craggy coastline is washed by spuming breakers, while the hills rise towards the Blue Mountains are buried under tumbles of bright-purple plumbagos and flaming heliconias.

The north coast centers on Ocho Rios, long one of the island's most popular vacation spots. Ochi, as Jamaicans call it, spells beaches, water sports, good dining and entertainment, as well as glorious waterfalls and botanical gardens.

The shoreline is lined with cascades, such as Dunn's River Falls, an indelible image of Jamaica that is guaranteed to elicit *ooohs* and *aaahs*. When you tire of the beach, you can drive through lushly majestic Fern Gully, admire the orchids and native flowers in botanical gardens, or take an open-air jitney or even a horseback ride through working plantations.

In its heyday, the north coast was a center of sugar production. Brimmer Hall and Prospect Plantation are popular excursion stops that still buzz with activity. Other historic properties, such as Greenwood, near Falmouth, and the site of Seville Nueva, near St Ann's, have been restored as museums. One, Good Hope, has even been given a new lease of life as a resplendent hotel in the country.

The region offers many superlative drives. The road inland from Falmouth to Good Hope, for example, leads to the edge of Cockpit Country – a beautiful and virtually inaccessible jungle-clad region of towering conical hillocks and

deep depressions.

Following the road south from Runaway Bay brings you to reggae star Bob Marley's mausoleum at his birthplace in the hills.

East of Ocho Rios the forests thicken. Just down the coast at Oracabessa novelist Ian Fleming dreamed up James Bond, and his adventure scenes from *Dr No* were shot hereabouts. Signs point the way to Firefly, dramatist Noel Coward's

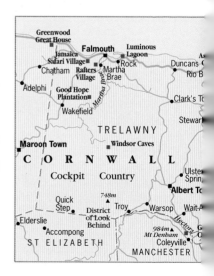

holiday retreat atop a high promontory above Port Maria. Coward asked to be buried here; you can visit, and understand why.

Runaway Bay, too, is evolving rapidly as a tourist resort. Its beach and inviting waters explain why. And sleepy Falmouth, which once buzzed with commerce, retains some of Jamaica's best-preserved historical gems, as well as a unique natural curiosity – a phosphorescent lagoon!

The active will find much to enjoy. Chukka Cove Equestrian Centre offers scenic horseback trails, plus polo. There are championship golf courses and water sports aplenty. You can raft the Martha Brae River. The north coast also boasts some of the best diving and snorkeling in Jamaica; scuba divers might even explore for the remains of two worm-ridden ships that Columbus is thought to have scuttled at Seville Nueva.

Climbing up the Dunn's River Falls

NORTH COAST JAMAICA

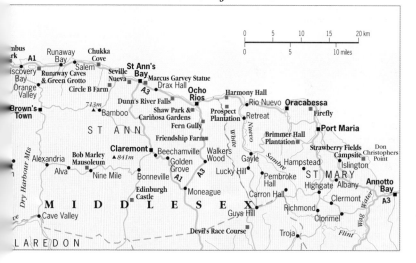

Ocho Rios

*O*cho Rios, 67 miles east of Montego Bay, anchors Jamaica's north coast. It is a 1½-hour drive from Mo'Bay, and a similar jaunt from Kingston over the central mountains. The rambling resort and lively harbor town lies at the foot of an escarpment and enjoys a serene mountain backdrop.

The town wraps around Ocho Rios Bay, which is rimmed by broad beaches. Its position is important – Ochi is a crossroads village where the coast road intersects the road to Moneague and Kingston. Its name, too, is a crossroads – of English and Spanish. Ocho Rios is not Spanish for "eight rivers," as its name suggests. Rather it is a corruption of the Spanish word *chorreras* – "the waterfalls." In 1657 a Spanish expeditionary force clashed with the English at a site they called Las Chorreras (assumed to be Dunn's River Falls). By 1800 records show the settlement here was officially known as Chorreras; and by 1841 as Ocho Rios.

In the 19th century Ocho Rios was a center for pimento production and export. Later years saw decline until assuaged by the arrival of cruise ships and a handful of luxury hotels in the 1960s.

Across the bay is an irrepressibly ugly dock (a now virtually abandoned bauxite-loading facility) where the cruise ships put passengers ashore. Dozens visit every month. Then seagoing sightseers storm ashore and overload the restaurants and tourist attractions. Cruise ships tend not to visit on weekends. Check the schedule with the Ocho Rios Tourist Office *(tel: (809) 974–2582)*.

Ocho Rios is small enough to stroll in 1 or 2 hours, with time added for browsing the native craft stalls. The town, some say, has been hit hard by overdevelopment. It is unkempt. Traffic jams are frequent. And hotels shoulder right up to the in-town beaches, which are sadly no longer backed by palms. Only occasional hints of sand can be observed as you stroll.

There is not much to see in Ochi, which has little charm and contains only one historic site: the diminutive fort, built in 1777 to defend the town against seafaring invaders. Turtle and Mallard's Beaches more than compensate with their shimmering white sands. The town is, however, heaven for shoppers. The roadsides are lined with craft stalls (yes, the vendors can be pushy!), and rows of duty-free shops sell everything from Swiss watches to *risqué* swimwear.

Portico Plantation Inn

Ocho Rios and its bay, as seen from Shaw Park Gardens

The town also offers a good choice of nightlife for the party crowd (more sedate bars proffer piano, Caribbean theme shows, and even karaoke). The choice among restaurants is good – everything from pizza to jerk pork. Ochi also boasts a widely varied style of hotels, including self-catering villas in the hills above the town and a selection of de-luxe all-inclusive resorts that are worlds unto themselves. Perched atop their own secluded bays are some of the finest traditional resort hotels in the whole of the Caribbean.

Ocho Rios is a good base for excursions farther afield – not least, Dunn's River Falls, which no one should miss.

The Jamaica Tourist Board, Ocean Village Shopping Centre, Ocho Rios (tel: (809) 974–2570/2582) can provide information and maps.

OCHO RIOS

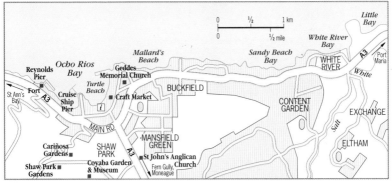

Wood carvings for sale in a shop at Dunn's River Falls

Carinosa Gardens

Lush and landscaped Carinosa is one of Ochi's three breathtaking botanical gardens. The 20-acre paradise is replete with cascading waterfalls, a walk-in aviary, orchid and fern gardens, and lily ponds. "New Jamaican" cuisine is served al fresco at a restaurant that seems to float on a pond created by a magnificent 40-foot waterfall.

Off the A3 (opposite the Parish Library), Ocho Rios. Tours. Open: daily, 9am–5pm. Admission charge.

Coyaba Gardens and Museum

Coyaba is the Arawak name for paradise. Strolling through these tropical gardens bursting with native flora you may well think you have arrived! You are never far from the mellifluous sound of waterfalls, and fish-filled ponds provide added amusement.

The Spanish-style museum provides an insight into Jamaica's cross-cultural influences and displays the history of Jamaica from Arawak days to post-emancipation. An art gallery displays the works of Jamaica's best creative talent.

There is a craft shop and a bar serving homemade ginger beer.

Adjacent to Shaw Park Gardens, off the A3 (tel: (809) 974–6235). Open: daily, 8:30am–5pm, Sundays, 8:30am–4:30pm. Admission charge.

Dunn's River Falls

Ocho Rios's most enticing attraction cascades over slippery wedding-cake tiers of limestone to the beach. Joining the daisy chain of tourists who link arms for the 600-foot climb to the top is a must. It is strenuous but well worth the extra effort. It's a good idea to hire one of the sure-footed guides.

Rubber-soled wading shoes also can be rented. Remember to take your bathing suit! The roadside ticket booth is at beach level.

The falls are considered the "Niagara of the Caribbean" – a gross exaggeration, but nonetheless they are exhilarating fun and splendidly photogenic.

Atop the falls woodcarving souvenir shops display some of the island's best examples of craftsmanship.

On the A3, 2 miles west of town (tel: (809) 974-2857). Open: daily, 9am-5pm, 8am–5pm on "ship" days. Admission charge.

Fern Gully

No visit to Ochi is complete without a drive up this sun-dappled road located a couple of miles south of town. The spectacular 3-mile journey leads uphill through a world of tropical ferns.

The road follows a dry riverbed that was planted with over 550 native varieties of ferns in the late 19th century. The lush ferns are threatened by noxious traffic fumes that are trapped beneath a canopy of 30-foot-tall fern trees.

Fern Gully is now a protected preserve. You may photograph – but no touching, please!

Ocho Rios Fort

The pocket-sized battery with four cannons *in situ* sits next to the disused bauxite-loading terminal west of the town. The fort (built in 1777) did brief duty as a slaughterhouse before being restored in the 1970s by Reynolds Jamaica Mines Ltd.

Shaw Park Gardens

It is a toss-up which is of greater appeal – the superb views over Ocho Rios or the botanical gardens brimming with exotic and native trees and shrubs. The trills

and squawks of birds resound pleasingly. The 25-acre attraction swathes the high ground south of town and was originally an attraction of the old Shaw Park Hotel, long since gone.

It is one of the most photogenic spots on the island. The 1-mile climb to the gardens affords spectacular vistas along the coast.

The gardens are sited on an erstwhile Arawak settlement, and a well-preserved Indian skeleton was found in 1763. Something of Arawak culture can be learned at the Coyaba Museum, adjacent to the gardens.

Off the A3, opposite the Public Library, 1 mile uphill (tel. (809) 974-2552). Open: daily, 9am-5pm. Admission charge.

Water cascading through exotic plants in Shaw Park Botanical Gardens

ARAWAK CAVES

These caves, 2 miles west of Rio Bueno, once provided shelter for Arawak Indians. There are vaulted chambers with Indian petroglyphs and artifacts, plus intriguing stalactite and stalagmite formations.

Admission free, but guides charge.

BOB MARLEY MAUSOLEUM

A revered site for Rastafarians and reggae fans, the resting-place of reggae superstar Bob Marley is fittingly located at his birthplace, Nine Miles, 15 miles south of Runaway Bay. He died of brain cancer on 11 May 1981.

Zion, the hilltop site of the mausoleum, is where Marley lived as a child. Its preferential position commands dramatic views over the hillocky, forest-clad mountains. The small hut, originally of wood, was rebuilt in stone when the musician was laid to rest. On its walls are

the words "I Bob love jah on love." Behind the hut is Marley's "inspiration stone," where he sat and made music and occasionally slept (as recorded in his song "Rock was my Pillow").

The mausoleum – a tall, oblong block of white Italian marble – is housed in a tiny church of Ethiopian design, surrounded by avocado and mango trees supposedly planted by the young Marley (the family moved to Kingston when he was 13 years old). The rising sun shines on the mausoleum through a stained-glass Star of David window. The interior is decorated with Marley paraphernalia: photos, paintings, "Ban the Bomb" and "One Love" stickers, and the like. A tattered black leather book contains thousands of signatures of those in the funeral procession, which reportedly stretched for 50 miles. As you turn the pages, the tears may well!

Artistic hands have graced everything – hut, mausoleum, inspiration stone – in Rasta colors: yellow for sunshine, green for nature's lushness, red for blood.

Flags flutter at the entrance to reggae legend Bob Marley's Mausoleum at Zion

A cheerful worker picks coconuts at Brimmer Hall Plantation

Marley sang of the oneness of humankind, epitomized by his words "one blood, one love" stressing that the sameness of human blood speaks of the equality of all races regardless of gender or skin color.

Immediately when you arrive you will be set upon by prospective guides and hustlers, but persevere. A gift shop is full of Marley paraphernalia.
Tel: (809) 999–7003. Open: daily. Admission charge.

BRIMMER HALL

This venerable wooden Great House, near Bailey's Vale, south of Port Maria, is the centerpiece of Brimmer Hall Plantation. The 700-acre farm culls bananas, coconuts, sugarcane, citrus, and pimento from the lush earth. A 1-hour guided tour by tractor-powered, canopied jitney teaches all about plantation life (intriguing esoterica include how many uses there are for coconuts, and how banana-tree stems are turned into women's stockings).

The white-walled house, built about 1817, has an impressive interior. Inside is as cool as a well. Dark hardwoods abound, along with Chinese inlaid hardwood tables, oriental rugs, and even an original suit of armor.

You may relax by the swimming pool, where you can sample tropical drinks, curried goat, ackee and salt fish, and other Jamaican treats. Gift shop.
Brimmer Hall, Port Maria (tel: (809) 994–2309). Tours 11am, 1:30, and 3:30pm. Admission charge. 4 miles southwest of Port Maria.

CARDIFF HALL

This 18th-century Great House is acclaimed, thanks to a restoration by the Duke of Newcastle. The gateway is flanked by guardhouses with pepperpot roofs. The vast estate was granted to one of Jamaica's first British settlers. A walled burial ground behind the house contains graves dating back to 1746.

At the time of writing the site was being developed as a resort.
Cardiff Hall (tel: (809) 973–2192). 1 mile east of Runaway Bay.

COCKPIT COUNTRY

Cockpit Country, a virtually townless territory, spreads through southern Trelawny Parish, south of Falmouth. It is an extraordinarily wild and stirringly beautiful region of looming hummocks and flat-bottomed depressions.

Cockpit Country is a classic case of karst topography – where a limestone plateau is dissolved to form deep sinkholes, the "cockpits" that give the region its name – covering some 500 square miles encircled by mountains. The region is riddled with caves that lie dangerously hidden beneath the undulating carpet of thick vegetation.

During colonial days Maroons – runaway slaves – found refuge here and fought the British to a standstill. Today the Cockpits are ringed by remote hamlets with peculiar names.

The forebidding region is the least explored in the country. No roads pierce beyond its fringe, though a few make penetrating stabs. Determined hikers can access the region with guides from Maroon Town, Accompong, and Quick Step, in the West. Hiking here is extremely rough.

Windsor Caves

On the northern edge of the Cockpits, about ½ mile south from Windsor Great House, is Windsor Caves. The inconspicuous opening gives no appreciable hint of the grandeur of the chambers within.

The limestone caves are full of stalagmites, stalactites, and flowing formations folded like stiff silken drapery. The passageways meander for 2 miles. Rooms range from cavernous to a tight fit. You grope your way forward with a guide who lights your way with a bamboo torch. Cavers can follow a stream that is the source of the Martha Brae.

Take a deep breath before entering – the bat manure gives off quite a stench! The caves are reputedly owned by Lady Rothschild (of the banking family), an entomologist who bought them to study the bats. They rush out at sunset.
No regular opening hours. Admission free, but guides charge a fee.

COLUMBUS PARK

Columbus Park, 1 mile west of Discovery Bay, marks the site where the famous explorer supposedly first set foot

The eerie Windsor Caves are some of the largest in Jamaica – well worth a visit

on Jamaica in 1494. The park, an open-air museum, enjoys a superb bluff-top setting overlooking the white-sand-fringed Discovery Bay.

The museum has various historical memorabilia – anchors, cannons, nautical bells, an old waterwheel in (albeit creaky) working condition, sugar-boiling "coppers," and a diminutive locomotive with a 20hp diesel engine that hauled sugarcane at Innswood Estate until 1969. There is also a beautiful mural depicting Columbus's landing.

Craft stalls west of the park offer good bargains.

The town of Discovery Bay is dominated by a bauxite-loading port just west of town.

1 mile west of Discovery Bay. Open: all day, daily. Admission charge.

EDINBURGH CASTLE

Some 3 miles south of Bonneville on the road from Claremont, at Pedro, is the hilltop ruin of Edinburgh Castle. Two loopholed walls and circular towers are all that remain of the once macabre site where a sadistic Scot named Lewis Hutchinson murdered more than forty innocent passersby in cold blood in the 1760s.

He is reputed to have decapitated his victims and tossed them into a sinkhole, but no bodies were ever found. The madman was caught while escaping to the sea and was promptly hanged.

MAROONS

When the English seized the island in 1655, the Spanish fled, and their slaves, free at last, took to the mountains, where they evolved their own culture. For a century and a half these Maroons (derived from the Spanish *cimarones* from *cima*, meaning peak, as both runaway animals and escaping slaves headed for the mountains) proved a thorn in the side of the English.

The Leeward Maroons lived in the Cockpit Country; the Windward Maroons occupied the Blue Mountains. Led by an Ashanti chief named Cudjoe, they launched a war against the British that was to last many decades (1690–1739). The Windwards joined them, led by a priestess named Nanny.

Using ruthless guerrilla tactics and assisted by the formidable terrain (Cockpit Country became known as the Land of Look Behind because English soldiers moved back-to-back to avoid ambush), the Maroons harassed the English until the latter gave up. In 1739 the British signed a peace treaty that granted the Leeward Maroons legal autonomy. In exchange the Maroons agreed to cease their hostilities and to refuse sanctuary to runaway slaves. They also agreed to assist the British in suppressing future slave rebellions.

A Second Maroon War erupted in 1795 when two runaway slaves who the Maroon's had handed over to the English authorities were used to flog two Maroons sentenced for stealing pigs. The 5 month war that ensued engulfed the island. Dogs and Indian trackers were eventually imported to track the Maroons, who finally surrendered. Eventually 600 Maroons were deported to Sierra Leone, becoming the first New World Africans to be repatriated to Africa.

Today little remains of Maroon culture.

A thriving port in the 18th century, Falmouth has plenty to interest

FALMOUTH

Ramshackle maybe, but still the best preserved Georgian town in Jamaica, and well worth 2 hours' peregrination. The bustling activity on Saturday is a reminder of the days when the town grew wealthy trading in sugar, slaves, and rum.

Traces of Falmouth's former elegance are concentrated along Market Street, west of Water Square. The street was used in the filming of *Papillon*. Many houses have Regency-style, wrought-iron balconies and a projecting upper story supported on columns to form a piazza at street level.

Points of interest include the Palladian courthouse (a replica of the original building dating back to 1817); the Methodist manse; the cut-stone warehouses of Hampden Wharf; the Phoenix foundry, one of the earliest industrial buildings in Jamaica; and the parish church, built in 1796. The William Knibb Memorial Church, at the corner of George and King Streets, commemorates the local Baptist minister whose work was fundamental in the abolition of slavery.

Seaboard Street is still a place to watch the local fishermen bring in their nets.

23 miles east of Montego Bay.

FIREFLY

The priceless panorama did not inspire the song "A Room with a View" – the song was composed in Hawaii in 1928 – but the vistas from Firefly, Sir Noel Coward's holiday retreat, are as staggering as any in Jamaica. The house, built atop a high promontory above Port Maria, is now a museum that looks as it did when the great playwright and novelist died here in 1973.

Coward discovered the site while vacationing with a friend in 1948. Driving around one day they arrived on a wide plateau where they settled down to paint until dusk, when huge luminous fireflies – locally called "peeny-wollies" or "winkies" – appeared. Coward immediately bought the property and 8 years later moved into the beloved home he built there.

Sean Connery, Laurence Olivier and Vivien Leigh, Roald Dahl and Patricia Neal, John Gielgud, David Niven, Peter Sellers, and other stars of screen and theater were all regular guests. Friends would say: "These martinis are very strong!" Coward would reply: "No, no! It's the altitude."

Coward lies buried beneath a white marble slab at the spot where he sat with so many illustrious friends, drink in hand, watching the sunset reflected on the long vista of coastline.

Firefly was given to the Jamaica National Heritage Trust in 1976, and it sadly fell into neglect. Today it is administered on behalf of the Trust by Island Outpost, which restored the house to look as it did on Sunday, 28 February 1965, the day the Queen Mother came to lunch.

Coward's brightly colored paintings are displayed in his studio; the former garage has been turned into a screening room with a spellbinding video of Coward's life? The interior of the simply furnished house looks like a set from one of his plays, with his two pianos back-to-back in the music room. Upstairs is Coward's so-called "room with a view," open on one side, and his bedroom containing his Jamaican pineapple four-poster and a closet full of Hawaiian shirts and silk pajamas.

The stone hut that is now a gift shop and restaurant serving afternoon tea was once a lookout post for lieutenant-governor of Jamaica Henry Morgan.

Fireflies still glow at nightfall.
PO Box 38, Port Maria, St Mary (tel: (809) 997–7201). Open: 8:30am–5:30pm. Admission charge. 2 miles south of Port Maria.

GREEN GROTTO

The unassuming entrance to Runaway Caves gives no hint of the scale and grandeur of the mysterious subterranean world within. A 45-minute tour is highlighted by a boat ride on the eerie, underground Green Grotto Lake, where the stalactites are reflected in crystal-clear water some 160 feet beneath the surface.

Your guide may make the formations chime by striking them with a stick. Spanish troops were thought to have hidden here before fleeing to Cuba in 1655.
2 miles west of Runaway Bay. Tours run hourly, 9am–5pm. Admission charge.

Elegant in death as in life, Noel Coward's grave at Firefly

Gracious living at Good Hope, now a luxury hotel

GOOD HOPE

Six miles south of Falmouth is an unpretentious Georgian Great House surrounded by meadows and well-tended orchards of coconut palms, papaya, and ackee.

Good Hope was built in 1755 and grew to be the node of the largest plantation empire in Jamaica (owner John Tharp eventually owned more than 10,000 acres and 3,000 slaves). The estate produced sugar until 1904; then it fell into disrepair.

It was recently magnificently restored and reborn in 1993 as a luxurious hotel. Good Hope maintains a stable of horses, and trails lead through the 2,000-acre working plantation. It is open for tours.

The house has many Palladian details and Adam friezes, plus a beautiful formal entrance with a double staircase and a columned portico. Among the other well-preserved 18th-century structures

are the Slave Hospital and the Counting House, plus parts of the aqueduct and sugar mill with a waterwheel.
PO Box 50, Falmouth, Trelawny (tel: (809) 954–3289).

HARMONY HALL

Harmony Hall, a large Victorian manor with green shingle roof and fretwork arches, 4 miles east of Ocho Rios, was built as a Methodist manse with an adjoining pimento estate. Today it is a showcase for the best of Jamaican arts and crafts.

The Back Gallery displays works by many of Jamaica's most illustrious artists; the Intuitive Room displays Primitive, Naive, and Folk art. Special exhibitions are mounted in the Front Gallery from mid-November to Easter.

Downstairs a gracious restaurant harks back to the 1920s.
P O Box 192, Ocho Rios (tel: (809) 975–

4222). On the coast road, 4 miles east of Ocho Rios. Admission free.

JAMAICA SAFARI VILLAGE

A crocodile farm unique to the Caribbean. There is a bird sanctuary and petting zoo, and those with the nerve can handle live snakes.

Tel: (809) 954–3065. Open: daily, 8:30am–6pm. Admission charge. 2 miles west of Falmouth.

LUMINOUS LAGOON

Agitate the waters at Rock, 2 miles east of Falmouth, and they seem to explode. The bay, also known as Luminous Lagoon, contains one of the world's largest concentrations of bioluminescent micro-organisms. These tiny creatures light up and glow ghostly green when disturbed. Fish swimming by shine eerily. Past development almost destroyed the creatures, but today they are making a comeback.

The bay is enclosed by mangroves.

Boats can be rented at the jetties. A night cruise departs from Fisherman's Inn *(tel: (809) 974–5317).*

MARTHA BRAE RIVER

This river rises from a subterranean chamber in the Cockpit Country and flows south to emerge on the coast at Falmouth. It is popular for raft trips that begin at Rafter's Village, 2 miles south of town.

River Raft Ltd, P O Box 547, Montego Bay (tel: (809) 952-0889).

ORACABESSA

Oracabessa is a sleepy, erstwhile banana port where dugout canoes still pull up on the beach. The village, on the A3, 13 miles east of Ocho Rios, is more famous as a film setting for *Dr No*, the first of the

James Bond movies – appropriately, since novelist Ian Fleming conjured up the ace of spies while writing here.

The origin of Oracabessa is obscure. Some say the name is derived from an Arawak Indian word, *juracabes*. Others say Columbus named the place because of the glow of the sun's rays on the headland – from *oro* (gold) and *cabeza* (head).

Goldeneye

Fleming wintered at his villa, Goldeneye, between 1946 and 1964. He wrote all thirteen Bond novels here. Fleming named his hero after the author of the ornithological classic *Birds of the West Indies*. Graham Greene, Truman Capote, Evelyn Waugh, and Fleming's neighbor, Sir Noel Coward, were frequent guests.

The house has gateposts topped by bronze pineapples. Within it contains much 007 memorabilia.

The beachfront house is privately owned and not open to the public. However it can be rented *(tel. (809) 994–2282).*

Follow the lane from the Esso sign towards the sea.

Some of the lively paintings on display at the Harmony Hall galleries

BIRDS OF JAMAICA

Jamaica has 252 species of birds, 26 of them indigenous. Their songs and gay plumage brighten every tourist's day.

The national bird – the red-billed streamertail hummingbird, or "doctor bird" – ranges from sea level to Blue Mountain Peak. The male's vivid, shimmering green-blue livery and scissor-shaped, sweeping tail appear everywhere, even on the Jamaican dollar bill and as the logo of Air Jamaica. Why "doctor bird"? Apparently the streamertail's long, needle-like beak resembles the lancets of doctors of old.

Smallest of Jamaica's four hummingbird species is the tiny vervain, or bee hummingbird; the brightest is the iridescent, rainbow-hued mango hummingbird.

A familiar bird is the kling kling, or shiny-black, pearly eyed Antillean grackle, a kleptomaniac that scavenges food from restaurant tables. The wrinkled, bald, bright-red head of the John Crow, too, is seen everywhere. According to local lore, this buzzard is named after the Revd John Crow, who would spread his black gown like the wings of a bird and become so impassioned during his sermons that his face and neck turned red above his black collar.

Two species of parrots, the flamboyant green-black and the yellow-billed, screech and chatter from their perches high in the lowland forest. There are bright-colored parakeets and finches, too.

The montane forests are filled with the mournful cries of the rufus-throated solitaire and the harsh cries of the red-headed Jamaican woodpecker. The plaintive call of the patoo (the screech or white owl) supposedly signals impending bad luck.

Kling kling (above), doctor bird (right), and John Crow (far right)

Flycatchers abound, including the loggerhead kingbird, whose black head bears a concealed yellow crown that can be raised when angry. More beautiful still is the indigenous wren-sized Jamaican tody, also known as "robin redbreast" or "Rasta bird." It makes its nest underground.

Of the seabirds terns and booby birds return seasonally to nest on outlying coral cays. Pelicans, too, are commonly seen, while frigate birds, with their hooked beaks and sinister forked tails, are easily seen soaring like kites on invisible strings.

Rocklands Bird Feeding Station (see page 108) is an excellent place to get face to face with Jamaica's most notable birds.

PORT MARIA

About 21 miles east of Ocho Rios the A3 sweeps around Galina Point to unveil a majestic, jade-colored bay, stupendously framed by mountains, with Blue Mountain Peak rising behind. Port Maria stretches along the bayfront.

This small and shabby town, much decayed since its heyday as a thriving banana port, awaits the tourism development that has so far passed it by, despite the beautiful setting.

Of interest, however, is St Mary's Parish Church at the west end of town, built of stone in 1861 with a churchyard shaded by palms. The ruin across the street is the former police station, destroyed by fire in 1988. Stop, too, at the 1820 courthouse, where you will find the Tacky Monument commemorating the leader of the Easter Slave Rebellion of 1760, which began at the Frontier Estate, east of town.

You can plant a tree yourself at Prospect Plantation

Before leaving take time to relax on Pagee Beach where you can swim safely and even play dominoes with the local fishermen, who may be persuaded to take you out to Cabarita Island.

PROSPECT PLANTATION

Prospect Plantation, 3 miles east of Ocho Rios, is a working plantation, redolent with tropical fruits. A covered-jitney ride (and horseback trails for the more active) winds past groves of coffee, cocao, citrus,

banana, and pimento, the aromatic allspice used in Jamaican seasoning. Only pimento and lime are grown commercially; the rest are for show.

Many famous world figures have planted commemorative trees, including Sir Winston Churchill, dramatist Sir Noel Coward, comedian Sir Charles Chaplin, and Prince Phillip. For $50 you, too, can plant a tree, which will be maintained for life.

A guided tour includes a peek inside the chapel of Prospect College, a magnificent stone structure with an old timbered roof. The college prepares boys to enter the defence and police forces. Alas, the striking 18th-century Great House (fortified with loopholes against raids by pirates) is not open for public viewing. Horseback rides are offered. *Tel: (809) 974–2373. Tours Monday–Saturday, 10:30am, 2pm, and 3:30pm; Sunday, 11am, 1:30pm, and 3pm.*

RIO BUENO

Most historians agree that this pretty, horseshoe-shaped bay at the mouth of the Rio Bueno is where Columbus first landed in Jamaica in 1494, having been chased from St Ann's Bay by hostile Indians. Today an unspoiled fishing village marks the spot. Old stone homes and warehouses line the main street, used as a setting for the film *A High Wind in Jamaica*.

St Mark's Anglican Church is pleasingly photogenic, sitting at the water's edge within a walled churchyard, its gateway overgrown with oleander and frangipani.
16 miles east of Falmouth.

Rio Bueno: Christopher Columbus was here – 500 years ago

RIO NUEVO

This site, 7 miles east of Ocho Rios, marks the spot where the Spanish governor, Don Cristobal Ysassi, was defeated by Oliver Cromwell's soldiers in June 1658.

You would never guess the site's historical importance but for the marker that reads: "On this ground on June 17, 1658, was fought the battle of Rio Nuevo to decide whether Jamaica would be Spanish or English. On one side were the Jamaicans of both black and white races, whose ancestors had come to Jamaica from Africa and Spain 150 years before. On the other side were the English invaders. The Spanish forces lost the battle and the island. The Spanish whites fled to Cuba but the black population took to the mountains and fought a long and bloody guerrilla war against the English. This site is dedicated to all of them."

Another memorial stands at the site of the old Spanish stockade near the mouth of the river. Sit awhile on the benches under shady pimento (allspice) trees and take in the fine view.

A Runaway Bay shopkeeper is pleased to offer conch shells and wood carvings for sale

with images of Columbus's three caravels. It was cast in his native city, Genoa.

The town is more famous, however, as the birthplace of national hero Marcus Garvey, born 17 August 1887. A larger-than-life statue of Garvey, considered the father of black nationalism in Jamaica, stands outside the St Ann's Parish Library.

In 1919 Garvey moved to the USA, having founded the Universal Negro Improvement Association (UNIA). His calls for self-reliance stirred black consciousness. He launched a steamship company, the Black Star Line, to repatriate blacks to Africa. Garvey was even elected provisional president of Africa at an international convention in New York in 1920. The white establishment gaoled him on false charges, thereby destroying his movement. Garvey died in London in 1940.

St Ann's Baptist Church, founded in 1827, faces an old, tumbledown market topped by a pretty wooden clock tower. The 1866 courthouse, on the main street next to the Parish church, is interesting for its pedimented porch. To the east is the old English fort, built of stone blocks hauled from Seville Nueva. It was abandoned in 1795 and used as a gaol. It still has iron grilles in the windows.

St Ann's prettiest structure is Our Lady of Perpetual Help Church, at the west end of the town. This little gem is of Spanish design and festooned with climbing plants. Palms lead through beautifully landscaped grounds.

7 miles west of Ocho Rios.

RUNAWAY BAY

Runaway Bay is touted as the place where Spanish forces fled Jamaica for Cuba after the decisive battle with the British in 1658. The name is more likely derived from the traffic in runaway slaves, who were harbored by illegal Spanish traders using this area for runs to Cuba.

Today escapees arrive here for sunning, diving, and golf. The town is virtually nonexistent, though there are several all-inclusive hotels and many villas, plus a superb golf course that is the site of Jamaica's oldest golf tournament, the annual Jamaica Pro-Am, held each November.

17 miles west of Ocho Rios. Open: daily, 9am–5pm. Admission charge.

ST ANN'S BAY

At this site explorer Christopher Columbus first arrived at Jamaica on 5 May 1494. He named the bay Santa Gloria "on account of the extreme beauty of its country" before sailing away. A bronze figure of the explorer, on the A3 west of town, is inscribed

SEVILLE NUEVA

Half a mile west of St Ann's Bay the A3 runs through Seville Nueva, the first Spanish settlement in Jamaica.

On his fourth and last voyage to the New World in 1503, Columbus careened his two worm-eaten vessels, *Capitana* and *Santiago de Palos*, at this site. (The sunken ships are believed to lie offshore). Abandoned by the Spanish governor in Hispaniola, Columbus spent a year and 4 days stranded in St Ann's Bay.

A dirt road on the seaward side leads to the Columbus site, where a sign reads: "The first known Jamaicans, the Arawaks, encountered Columbus and the Spaniards on this property."

In November 1509 Don Juan de Esquivel, who had been with Columbus in 1494, returned and laid the foundations of Seville Nueva. The town, which included a fortress, church, and the first sugar mill in Jamaica, never prospered – it was built too close to the swamps. After 24 years the capital was transferred to Villa de la Vega, today's Spanish Town. Crumbling stone structures are all that remain of the early Spanish habitation (artifacts found here are now in the Institute of Jamaica).

In 1745 Richard Hemming, an officer in the Cromwellian army, despoiled the Spanish ruins to build the Seville Estate on the landward side of the highway. A road leads to the "busha" (overseer's) house, sugar mill, copra kiln, waterwheel, and boiling house. Seville Great House sits on the ridge above, with a commanding view over Seville Nueva.

Today the site is operated as a museum by the National Heritage Trust.

½ mile west of St Ann's Bay (tel: (809) 922–1287). Open: daily. Admission charge for the museum and Great House.

WHITE RIVER

This small river, 2 miles east of Ocho Rios, is popular for rafting, especially for the "Night on the White River" on weekends. Fishing boats and rafts gather at the river mouth, where there are several restaurants.

RIGHT EXCELLENT
MARCUS MOSIAH GARVEY
NATIONAL HERO
BORN AUGUST 17, 1887 – DIED JUNE 10, 1940
JAMAICA NATIONAL TRUST COMMISSION

Statue of Marcus Garvey at St Ann's Bay

Ocho Rios Drive

There is history and scenic beauty around every bend on this drive, combining coast and interior mountains. Inland the scenery opens up fully into sublime tableaus that will have you wishing for more. The route is well paved yet little traveled. *Allow 4–5 hours, including stops.*

Leave Ocho Rios westward on the A3, passing the remains of Ocho Rios fort on the right. After about 3 miles, turn left at Dunn's River Falls.

1 DUNN'S RIVER FALLS
Dunn's River tumbles 600 feet over wedding-cake tiers to the beach. Climb it with a guide. Alternatively a walkway lets you admire the view *(tel: (809) 974–2857. Open: daily, 9am–5pm, 8am–5pm on "ship" days. Admission charge)*.

Continue west along the A3 about 4 miles to St Ann's Bay. Leave the bypass and turn left into town; then left again for the parish library.

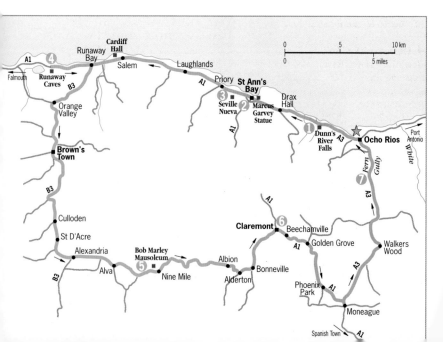

2 ST ANN'S BAY

Marcus Garvey, the father of black nationalism, was born in St Ann's in 1887. A commemorative statue to the national hero stands outside the parish library.

The A3 becomes the A1 west of St Ann's. Follow it 1 mile to Seville Great House and Heritage Park.

3 SEVILLE GREAT HOUSE AND HERITAGE PARK

Seville Nueva was the first Spanish settlement in the New World. Remnants of the fortifications and other structures still stand between the highway and the sea. Across the road is the Seville Estate and, on the ridge above, Seville Great House built in 1745. The site also has Arawak Indian remains. (See also page 85.)

Continue west. Runaway Caves are on the left, 2 miles beyond Runaway Bay.

4 RUNAWAY CAVES

Beautiful stalagmites and stalactites highlight these underground caverns. A guide may coax musical notes from the formations as you enjoy a boat ride through the Green Grotto. (See also page 84.)

Return to Runaway Bay. Turn right. The climbing road offers views back over the coast. After 4 miles turn left at Orange Valley. Continue to Brown's Town and Alexandria. Turn left at the police station. Follow the signs for the Bob Marley Foundation.

5 BOB MARLEY MAUSOLEUM

Reggae superstar Bob Marley lies buried at Nine Miles, a humble village where he

Landscape near Alexandria: typical of the glorious scenery on the Ocho Rios Drive

was born in 1945. Hustlers are heavy-handed, but a guided tour of Marley's childhood home and mausoleum is interesting.

Continue eastwards through a dramatic landscape of precipitous, jungle-clad hillocks and gorges and then bucolic countryside reminiscent of the Yorkshire Dales. Keep left at Y-junctions at Alderton and Bonneville. Continue to Claremont.

6 CLAREMONT

A somnolent crossroads town whose Wild West-style houses have wooden front sidewalks. A beautiful old clock tower sits in the center of town.

Turn right at the clock tower on to the A1. Moneague is 6 miles. Turn left onto the A3. After 9 miles descend through Fern Gully.

7 FERN GULLY

A serpentine road descends through this steep-sided gorge lined by lush ferns. Sunlight filters through the canopy, creating a kind of subaqueous light. Craft stalls line the road.

The West

*T*he West is neatly demarcated by the parishes of St James, Hanover, and Westmoreland. Together they offer virtually everything the visitor to Jamaica hopes for.

Montego Bay is the first place most visitors to Jamaica see. It offers a pretty fair sampling of what the island has to offer: stunning beaches; hotels of every description; lots of golf, tennis, and water sports; river rafting; intriguing history, including a working plantation and Great House; plus good nightlife, restaurants, and shopping.

The young at heart, regardless of age, head for Negril. This one-time haven for pirates and passing whalers and, later, for hippies, is today a haven of simple pleasures. It is as laid-back or as lively as you wish.

There's mo'fun, mo'sun, and mo'to do in Mo'Bay! Montego Bay, or "Mo'Bay" as locals call it, is Jamaica's biggest resort, with activities to suit every taste. Most of the options are based on the beach or are on, over, or under the crystalline waters of the recently created Montego Bay Marine Park, a 6,000-acre marine reserve that captivates water enthusiasts.

Broader pleasures await within a short drive of town. A bevy of plantation homes can be explored. Most well known is Rose Hall, an 18th-century mansion that is said to be haunted by the wicked "White Witch." Worth a look, too, are Belvedere and Croydon – both are working plantations. A short jaunt into the hills also leads to a bird feeding station, the German settlement of Seaford Town, and Frome and the sugar estates of the Westmoreland Plain. Speaking of sugar, do not miss a sojourn at the Appleton Rum Estate.

You can head off on your own along back roads that will give you a taste of the real Jamaica. Take your camera – the scenery is spectacular. Should you choose to explore *terra incognita* on foot, take a guide – the back country is a patchwork of illegal ganja (marijuana) plots. It is not a good idea to trespass!

Montego Bay's Cornwall Beach demonstrates the delights that the West has to offer

WEST JAMAICA

Nowhere better epitomizes Jamaica's "No problem, mon!" attitude than Negril, at the westernmost tip of the island. It is difficult not to fall right into its shrug-off-the-blues way of life. The beach seems endless. The calm waters are a palette of light blues and greens. And the consistently spectacular sunsets get more applause than the live reggae concerts for which Negril is famous.

The West is imbued with accommodations ranging from sophisticated, all-inclusive resorts to budget cottages and quaint bed-and-breakfast inns. Tryall and Half Moon deserve singling out as elegant resorts with their own championship golf courses counted among the most beautiful and challenging in the Caribbean.

Getting around is easy. Both Negril and Mo'Bay have a surfeit of scooters and motorbikes for rent. Rental cars are generally easy to come by (*do* book ahead), and day excursions are widely available.

MONTEGO BAY

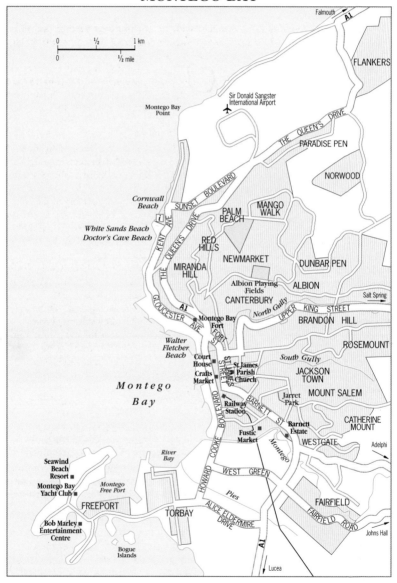

Montego Bay

*M*ontego Bay lures sun worshippers with its magnificent setting: an aquamarine bay surrounded by lush, green hills and fringed by soft, white sands. Jamaica's vacation hub flows over with things to do and places to see.

Like other tourist centers, however, Mo'Bay has bad mixed in with the good. Its street vendors, for example, are notoriously pushy. Fortunately the Jamaica Tourist Board is making far-reaching efforts to allay this. The following information will better acquaint you with whether Mo'Bay is for you.

Christopher Columbus dropped anchor here in 1494. Jamaica's first visitor named the bay The Gulf of Good Weather. No one disputes it. The town's start, however, was more ignominious – as the lard capital of the Caribbean. "Montego" derives from the Spanish word for hog fat, *manteca*. Wild boars in the hills supplied the lard. Later it became a major port for bananas and sugar. Many of the magnificent homes of the sugar barons remain.

Mo'Bay sprang to life as a spa resort in the early 1900s. The supposedly beneficial sea waters – and the beaches – are what started it all, especially Doctor's Cave Beach, where tourists and locals alike head on a typically beautiful day. Very few come today for a Doctor's Cave treatment, though everybody finds Mo'Bay just what the doctor ordered.

There are really two Montego Bays: the town center and the touristy hotel strip along Gloucester Avenue, north of the center. It is a mile-long walk between the two. Sadly the beaches are hidden from view for most of the way. What you would like to see lies beyond fencing. En route you pass the remains of Fort Montego, as dishevelled as the wasteland backing Walter Fletcher Beach. A crafts market here brims with bargains, as does the larger one at Howard Cooke Boulevard and Strand Street.

Downtown is a hive of activity. St James Street is the main thoroughfare. At its core is Sam Sharpe Square, which evokes sombre memories. Church Street is well worth a stroll for its cluster of historic buildings, including St James Parish Church. Fustic Market on Barnett Street is a whirligig of color and noise where the people of Mo'Bay do their shopping and gossiping. At the southernmost end of Barnett Street is the entrance to the Barnett Estate. This working plantation begs a visit.

Mo'Bay has Mo'Rooms – forty percent of all hotel rooms in Jamaica! – and restaurants that run the gamut from poor to superb. Pick from a string of options along Gloucester and Kent Avenues. Many of the best eateries are associated with the best hotels.

Mo'Bay's bevy of clubs and discos takes second place to the town's nocturnal beach parties, highlighted by a street festival each Monday night in which Gloucester Avenue is closed off and transformed into a *jonkanoo* carnival. Reggae Sumfest rocks the city in August, when the best of international and local reggae acts jam for 4 pulsating days. *The Jamaica Tourist Board office (tel: (809) 952–4425) is at Cornwall Beach. JTB information desks are also located at the airport and next to the public library at Fort Street and Howard Cooke Boulevard.*

Cornwall Beach, Montego Bay, has everything: sun, sea, sand – and hustlers!

Barnett Estate

This 3,000-acre estate is a living, breathing plantation on the edge of the city. At one time the estate encompassed most of Montego Bay and its environs.

Barnett was established by Colonel Nicolas Jarrett, who landed with the British expedition that took Jamaica from the Spanish in 1655. His progeny, the Kerr-Jarretts, still reside on and work the plantation, which produces sugar, bananas, mangos, papayas, and coconuts.

The estate was recently opened to the public, and there is a visitor center and museum. A tour leads you back in time and includes the former plantation manager's house and the fully furnished Old Great House on the brow of the hill, with a panoramic view over Montego Bay. You can watch a Chattanooga grind sugarcane in the old sugar mill.
Barnett Ltd, PO Box 876, Montego Bay
(tel: (809) 952-1709). Open: daily, 8:30am–5:15pm. The entrance is on Barnett Street. Admission charge.

Beaches

Montego Bay's handful of beaches all share the same pellucid waters and shimmering white sands. Several resorts pivot on their own private beaches. The public beaches are concentrated in the heart of the tourist strip, along Gloucester Avenue. Coral reefs grow just off shore and are easily seen by snorkeling or glass-bottom boating. Water sports are widely available.

The Seawind Beach, at Montego Freeport, has a nude section for those seeking an all-over tan.

Cornwall Beach:

Cornwall Beach has excellent bathing and water sports. It is marred by a coterie of locals hustling everything from

T-shirts to drugs. It was developed by the Jamaican Tourist Board, whose headquarters are here. A beach party is held here every Friday.

Tel: (809) 952–3463. Behind the Jamaican Tourist Board headquarters, opposite the Fantasy Hotel. Open: daily, 9am–5pm. Admission charge.

Doctor's Cave Beach:

Beloved by repeat visitors to Mo'Bay, this arc of sugar-white coral sand is credited with providing the genesis of Jamaica's tourist trade. It was once the property of an eccentric physician, Dr Alexander McCatty, who donated the beach to the city as a bathing club in 1906. A few years later an enterprising British physician popularized the sea waters here for their supposed curative powers, attracting tourists and a nucleus of small hotels that rose behind the beach.

Today it is administered by a board of prominent Montegonians as a private bathing club. Nonmembers are charged a small fee. There are changing-rooms and a bar.

Tel: (809) 952–2566. Opposite the Gloucestershire Hotel. Open: daily, 8:30am–5pm. Admission charge.

Walter Fletcher Beach:

Another public beach between the town center and the hotel enclave on Gloucester Avenue. It is named after a former Custos of St James (see **Politics**). You pass through an unwelcoming and unkempt lawn that locals tend to use as a garbage dump, but the beach is clean.

Facilities include changing-rooms, ice-cream bar, restaurant, and tennis courts.

Tel: (809) 952–2044. At the south end of Gloucester Avenue, opposite the fort. Open: daily, 9am–5pm. Admission charge.

This brass cannon at Montego Bay Fort was fired only twice

Montego Bay Fort

Virtually nothing remains of the bastion built in 1752 to protect Montego Bay. Three large brass cannons, green with patina, still point to sea. They were fired only twice: in 1760 to celebrate the capture of Havana when, alas, one blew up and killed the cannoneer; and in 1795, when the cannons were loosed at a British ship, the *Mercury*, which sailed in at dusk and was mistaken for a French privateer.

The fort is bisected by Fort Street. There is a crafts market on the leeward side.

Open: all day, daily. Admission free.

Old Georgian House

This attractive structure comprises two 19th-century Georgian homes separated by a paving stone courtyard. The merchant who built them supposedly housed his wife in one and his mistress in the other. Fully restored, they now house an art gallery and restaurant.

Tel: (809) 952–0632. At the corner of Union Street and Orange Street.

Eighteenth-century St James Parish Church reflects a more affluent and elegant age

St James Parish Church

St James Parish Church, built 1775–82, is regarded as one of the finest churches in Jamaica. The venerable building was constructed of limestone in the shape of a Greek cross. Note the deep cracks – a legacy of the devastating earthquake of 1 March 1957 (the church was extensively damaged, and then rebuilt in 1958).

Within are several marble monuments erected by the early sugar barons. One, by the famous English sculptor John Bacon (1740–99), is dedicated to Rose Palmer, the virtuous wife maligned in legend as the White Witch of Rose Hall (see page 106).

The palm-shaded churchyard contains graves dating back 200 years. Most are dilapidated, and some are so weathered as to be barely legible.

Sam Sharpe Square

Despite the island's seductive appeal, it is difficult to avoid her less savory history. Sam Sharpe Square, in the center of town, brims with slave-day memories.

The square is named after local Baptist minister "Daddy" Sam Sharpe, who led the Christmas Slave Rebellion of 1831. The British authorities reacted by hanging Sharpe in the square. He and 500 followers were strung four at a time on the gibbet.

When laid out in 1755 it was called The Parade and, later, Charles Square in honor of the then governor, Admiral Charles Knowles. Its centerpiece is a pretty bronze fountain (painted silver) on a roundabout; it functions intermittently and is dedicated to John Edward Kerr (1840–1903), who pioneered the local banana trade. Note the drinking troughs placed at varied heights to quench the thirst of human, horse, and dog.

The shell of the once-splendid Georgian courthouse, which burned down in recent times, commands the southwest corner.

The bustling square was spruced up in the mid-1980s and lavishly paved in stone. It is a gathering place for locals and a good place to sit and watch Jamaicans at work and play. You may chance upon a lively debate during periods of election fever, when the square is a center of political action.

Note the restored period structures occupied by Jamaica's leading banks.

The Cage:

The tiny antique building on the northwest corner dates back to 1806. Bars on the windows speak of its history as a gaol for runaway slaves and any blacks who on Sundays were found on the streets after 3pm. The tiny steeple contains a bell, rung at 2pm during slave days to warn blacks that the curfew would soon begin. The Cage has since found many uses, and at the time of writing houses a tour and ticket service.

Sam Sharpe Memorial:

Fronting The Cage is an impressive bronze statue of national heroes Paul Bogle and Sam Sharpe, the latter with bible in hand, addressing a rapt audience. The tableau of five bronze statues was unveiled in 1984.

Town House

This elegant Georgian town house is built of red brick brought as ballast from England. The house was built in 1765 by a wealthy merchant, David Morgan. It later served as the church manse, the house of a Jamaican governor's mistress, a Masonic lodge, and finally a hotel, when it occasioned a husband–lover confrontation, the legacy of which is a bullet hole in the mahogany staircase.

The house – now a law office with a popular restaurant in the basement – is festooned with rambling laburnum that climbs to the roof.

16 Church Street (tel: (809) 952–2660).

Sam Sharpe Square is quiet now but has seen troubled times in the past

ACCOMPONG

Accompong is the capital of the western Maroons, the recalcitrant society of escaped slaves and their descendants. It is a forbidding drive along deep-rutted, narrow roads that lead into the edge of the Cockpit Country.

The hamlet, 8 miles north of Maggotty, is little more than a string of shacks and small houses along the roadside. The Presbyterian Church is the sole structure of substance. A National Trust monument at the crossroads, or Parade Ground, commemorates Cudjoe, the Maroon leader who held the British Army at bay before signing the 1739 peace treaty that ratified the settlement at Accompong and ceded 1,000 acres to the Maroons.

Accompong is named after Cudjoe's brother. It is surrounded by scenery so marvellous that it is difficult to imagine that the area has such bitter memories.

The township still operates semi-autonomously under a town council headed by a "Colonel" elected by ballot (for many years the Jamaican government had no jurisdiction over the Maroons, except where the crime was murder). It is still considered respectful to pay a call on the Colonel. Locals may attempt to extract an entrance fee to the village.

On Treaty Day (6 January) the drums begin to beat, *abeng* horns trumpet loudly, animals are slaughtered for traditional feasts, and people flock from far and wide for the ensuing celebration.

APPLETON RUM ESTATE

You do not have to like rum to enjoy a visit to Jamaica's oldest and largest rum factory – the heart of a 4,400-hectare plantation that nestles in the breathtakingly beautiful valley of the Black River.

A tour of the distillery reveals the process by which J Wray and Nephew Ltd have been producing superb rums since 1749. King George III and George Washington apparently considered Appleton rums "the rum of choice." Some of the copper distillation pots still in use date back over a century.

Most visitors arrive on the popular Governor's Coach Tour (see **Getting Away From it All**), an organized excursion from the major resorts. Itinerants are also welcome. There is a hospitality lounge, plus gift shop, coffee shop, restaurant (advance orders only), and bar.

Jamaica Estate Tours, c/o Appleton Estate, Siloah, St Elizabeth (tel: (809) 997–6077). Open: daily, 9am–5pm, last tour 3:30pm. Admission charge. On the B6, 2 miles west of Siloah.

BELVEDERE ESTATE

The road south from Montpelier and Chester Castle leads to Belvedere, a family-owned 1,000-acre estate. The driveway passes through a lush plantation of bananas, citrus, and pineapple, green upon green.

You arrive at a rundown Great House and uniquely re-created post-Emancipation village. Pretty guides dressed in frilly dresses will demonstrate the use of an old sugar press pulled by a mule; then lead you through the village where latter-day craftsfolk and artisans – blacksmith, basket-weaver, coffee grinder, and the like – keep alive traditional skills.

A thatched restaurant offers traditional Jamaican fare. Take your pick of the tour: a guide will come in your car, or choose a tractor-pulled jitney.

Belvedere Estate, PO Box 361, Montego

_Bay (tel: (809) 952–6001). Open:
Monday–Saturday, 10am–4pm. Admission
charge._

BLACK RIVER

Black River, capital of St Elizabeth, is the
gateway to the south coast. It is one of
Jamaica's most peaceful towns, strung
along a jade-blue bay. Gingerbread
houses enhance the general charm of the
High Street, where old-style colonnaded
timber houses lead to the dock at the
river mouth. The river is stained dark as
molasses by minerals.

Marvel at the view from the bridge at
the river mouth, where fishing trawlers
gather, and ships are still loaded by
lighters, as they were in the 19th century
when a boom in the logwood trade

brought brief prosperity.

Two architectural highlights are the
porticoed courthouse and yellow-brick
church that face the water. The timber-
framed Waterloo Guest House was the
first building in Jamaica to install electric
lighting, in 1893.

_43 miles west of Mandeville, 31 miles east of
Savanna-la-Mar._

Black River: Mangroves reach into the water
(right), the Chamber of Commerce (below)

The Pier at Savanna-la-Mar, Jamaica

BLENHEIM

You could buzz through Blenheim with no hint that this hamlet was the birthplace of the Rt Excellent Sir Alexander Bustamante.

Perhaps the most colorful of Jamaica's many colorful political figures, Bustamante entered politics at the late age of 50 and worked assiduously on behalf of the poor and underprivileged. He founded the Jamaica Labour Party before becoming Jamaica's first prime minister in 1962.

His father, Robert Clarke, was an overseer on the Blenheim Estate. The thatched farm has been rebuilt by the National Trust and is now a national monument. A memorial service is held here annually on 6 August – the anniversary of Bustamante's death.
3 miles east of Davis Cove, 6 miles southwest of Lucea.

BLUEFIELDS BAY

The beautiful sweep of Bluefields Bay east of Savanna-la-Mar has long been popular – today with locals and the occasional tourist enamored of its wide, gently curving beach, and in times gone by with pirates who favored its good anchorage. Henry Morgan set sail from here in 1670 on his infamous raid on Panama. At Belmont Point, at the south end of the bay, is a fort built in 1767 by an estate owner as protection against pirates.

The shore is lined with jerk stands, and coconut vendors stalk the beach, which gets crowded during weekends and holidays.

These are prime fishing waters good for spiny lobsters and gamefish, such as tuna, bonito, and sailfish. You may still see local anglers in canoes hewn from cotton trees.

11 miles east of Savanna-la-Mar, 20 miles west of Black River.

BLUE HOLE PLANTATION

Blue Hole Plantation is located 1,200 feet up in the hills of St James. The estate grounds abound with fruit trees – mango, sour sop, ackee, pimento, and breadfruit. Lording over it all is a two-story stone-and-wood Great House with gingerbread trim, built by slaves for the Waite family in the early 18th century. The Waites had sided with Cromwell against King Charles and fled to Jamaica after the Restoration.

Attractions include a sugar mill and boiling house (partly destroyed in the slave rebellion of 1832), a reconstructed Arawak village, a craft village and herb garden, plus horse stables, a mini-zoo, restaurant, and bar.

Blue Hole Plantation, Little River, PO St James (tel: (809) 995–2070). Open: Monday to Sunday, 9am–4pm. Near Flower Hill, 6 miles east of Montego Bay.

CATADUPA

The charming railway village of Catadupa nestles on the deeply forested western fringe of the Cockpit Country. Coffee is grown locally and there is a small factory for washing and pulping coffee beans.

The hamlet was once a stop for the Appleton Express that operated until 1992 between Montego Bay and the Appleton Rum Factory. Catadupa's inhabitants derived much of their income from tailoring shirts and blouses for passengers, who were measured on the outbound journey and picked up the finished garment on the return. The tiny railway station still stands.

Catadupa is the Greek name for the Nile cataracts.
18 miles south of Montego Bay.

Croydon Estate

This 132-acre plantation on the outskirts of Catadupa grows coffee, pineapple, and citrus on steep, terraced hills. A "see, hear, touch, and taste" tour lets you sample tropical fruits in season, and you can watch coffee being processed.

National hero Sam Sharpe was born here. He rose to become a "daddy," or leader, of the native Baptists of Montego Bay and led the 1831 Slave Rebellion for which he was hanged. Sam Sharpe Square in Montego Bay is named for him.

Croydon can be visited on a ½-day tour from Montego Bay. A Jamaican barbecue lunch is included at a hilltop restaurant with inspirational views.
Tel: (809) 952–4137. Tours Tuesday, Wednesday, and Friday, 10am–3pm. Admission charge.

Enjoying a nice drink of coconut milk

ELDERSLIE

Elderslie, 8 miles north of Maggotty, bills itself as the "heart of the Cockpit Country," although it lies on the fringe. Its inhabitants dubiously also claim ancestry from the Maroons, the society of escaped slaves who lived in the Cockpits.

Less controversial is that it is home to some of Jamaica's leading woodcarvers, who skillfully handle mallets and chisels to craft subtle, delicate forms from blocks of lignum vitae.

While here peek inside the Wondrous Caves containing a small underground lake.

Wondrous Caves are located at Cook Bottom. Admission charge.

FROME

Frome is a sugar town set in a 60-square-mile alluvial plain that is one of the two largest sugar-producing areas in Jamaica. Frome Sugar Factory was for many years the largest in the West Indies. It was built in 1938 by the West Indies Sugar Company to process the sugar from their sixteen estates.

Neat rows of sugarcane near Frome

The factory's opening precipitated violent labor troubles when thousands of unemployed people migrated to the region seeking work. At that time men received only 15 cents a day for their labor; women were paid 10 cents. Labor activist Alexander Bustamante (see also **Blenheim**) became the champion of the workers' cause (and later Jamaica's first prime minister).

A monument in town celebrates "Labour Leader Bustamante and the workers for their courageous fight in 1938 on behalf of the working people of Jamaica."

Factory visits can be arranged by prior request *(tel: (809) 955–6080)*. A good time to visit is between November and June, during the sugar harvest.
5 miles north of Savanna-la-Mar.

GREAT RIVER

This moderate-sized river cuts a ravine that forms the boundary between St James and Hanover. It is a popular waterway for soothing 1-hour rafting trips from Lethe, a small mountain village with an old stone bridge built in 1828 and faithfully restored after it was toppled by the 1957 earthquake. The

The handsomely furnished dining room of Greenwood Great House

rapids are sufficient to rouse you from reverie. (See also **Getting Away from It All**).

Fishing enthusiasts may be tempted to cast for snook and tarpon in the river mouth, 12 miles west of Montego Bay.

GREENWOOD GREAT HOUSE

Greenwood Great House, 17 miles east of Montego Bay, was built in the 1790s as a guest house by the family of poet Elizabeth Barrett Browning. The Barretts came to Jamaica in the 1660s and grew immensely wealthy from their sugar estate.

The fieldstone and wood plantation-style home retains its historic ambience. Guides in plantation dress lead tours.

Greenwood is perhaps the finest antique museum in the Caribbean. Its marvels include the original library with rare books dating from 1697, plus oil paintings, Wedgwood china, musical instruments, a court jester's chair, a grisly mantrap (used for catching runaway slaves), and an inlaid rosewood piano given as a betrothal gift by Edward VII to his fianceé. Carriages, a hearse, and antique fire-fighting equipment are displayed in the gardens.

The long veranda on the north façade provides a breathtaking panorama of the Caribbean and Barrett's estate.
Greenwood Great House, PO Box 169, Montego Bay (tel: (809) 953–1077). Open: daily, 9am–6pm. Admission charge.

IPSWICH CAVE

Ipswich Cave, 19 miles north of Black River, is often inaccurately described as Jamaica's second-largest cave. Nevertheless the great vaulted chambers are cut deep into the limestone massif called the Cockpit Country, with galleries full of mesmerizing formations. Walkways lead through the well-lit caves.

The site was once a stop on the itinerary of the Appleton Express. The railway still passes by, but, alas, trains no longer run.

Local guides are on hand to rent their services.
No set opening hours. Admission free. Local guides charge a fee.

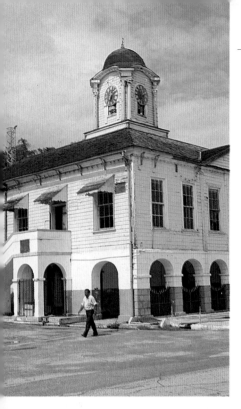

Lucea is proud of the unusual clock tower that surmounts its courthouse

identity. About 36,400 Indians came to Jamaica as indentured laborers after the abolition of slavery. Some 12,000 settled around Little London.

Conditions were hardly any better for the Indians than for the slaves. Mortality was so high that in 1914 the Indian government forbade further migration.

Curry brought from India is today a staple of Jamaican cuisine. The Indians also brought *ganja* (marijuana), now ubiquitous throughout the island.

7 miles west of Savanna-la-Mar, straddling a crossroads on the A2.

LUCEA

The once-prosperous sugar port is now a somnolent fishing harbor that springs to life only on market days. "Lucy" shelters on the western shore of a mile-wide harbor.

Despite its shabby appearance, architectural highlights include the 19th-century Georgian courthouse fronted by a fountain in the town square. The stone structure with arched veranda is topped by a wooden second story. Note the clock tower (about 1817) supported on pseudoCorinthian columns and supposedly modelled after the helmet of the German Royal Guard. A single family has had the job of keeping the clock in working order for over a century.

In the last century Lucea had many Jewish merchants. Their stores remain on Main Street, along with an old fireproof warehouse with an arched interior and double-barrel roof.

Peek inside the parish church (on the corner of Fort Charlotte Drive and the A1) to peruse monuments to prominent Jamaican personalities. Close by are the

KENILWORTH

This erstwhile sugar estate preserves the ruins of one of Jamaica's best examples of 17th-century industrial architecture.

A derelict Great House overlooks the remains of the massively constructed sugar mill and boiling house-cum-distillery. Note the large oval Palladian windows. A youth camp now occupies much of the estate.

The tomb of estate owner Thomas Blagrove (1733–55) claims "his humane treatment of his servants, in a region not abounding in such examples, induced their cheerful obedience."

LITTLE LONDON

This anachronism on the cultural landscape is heavily populated with East Indians, who retain much of their ethnic

remains of Fort Charlotte, which guards the harbor. The octagonal fortress retains three massive cannons on rotary carriages. A frigate bird colony nests on the cliff. Fort Charlotte, named after the wife of King George III, served time as a gaol for slaves. It now houses a school, the Hanover Museum, with a few meager exhibits and a craft workshop run by handicapped folk.
28 miles west of Montego Bay.

MAGGOTTY

This somnolent market town stretches along the banks of the Black River. An impressive waterfall, alas, was sacrificed to produce hydro-electric power. A bauxite-processing factory haunts the landscape; fortunately it is disused – no bad thing, for its effluvia polluted the river.
19 miles north of Black River.

Apple Valley Park *(tel: (809) 997–6000)*, on the riverbank in the center of town, features hiking trails, plus paddleboats on a pond good for fishing.

MAROON TOWN

Despite its name the hamlet of Maroon Town, 16 miles southeast of Montego Bay, did not remain a settlement of Maroons (escaped slaves and their descendants) for long. The British tired of attempting to suppress the Maroons and built a series of fortified barracks throughout the region. One such sits atop the former Maroon settlement of Trelawny Town, 1 mile east of Maroon Town. The remains of the encampment still can be seen.

MIDDLE QUARTERS

Middle Quarters, "shrimp capital of Jamaica," is a tiny village where women folk wait to waylay motorists with little pink bags full of the region's speciality – peppered shrimp. Stop to sample, but make sure you choose a vendor close to a bar shack selling very cold Red Stripe beer. The shrimp are drawn from local rivers using traps of split bamboo.
On the A2, 6 miles north of Black River.

The shrimp-sellers of Middle Quarters

NEGRIL

Negril is Jamaica's most laid-back resort – a place where virtually anything goes. Forget the sightseeing. Negril is for languorous sunning by day and bacchanalia by night.

Negril's star attraction is its stunning 7-mile-long beach that slopes gently into water the colors of jade. Negril was cut off from development (or protected, depending on your perspective) by crocodile-infested swamps until 1965, when the road link with Montego Bay, 52 miles away, was completed.

Negril quickly became a nirvana for those seeking an alternative lifestyle. Some visitors discovered "magic mushrooms" – hallucinogens – that are still available in raw form or in a local speciality, mushroom tea.

When a resort called Hedonism opened in 1977, tales of an uninhibited lifestyle launched Negril to fame. The mid-1980s saw a burst of hotel development that has not yet ended. Fortunately a strict building code has kept the resorts from growing taller than the palms that border the beach.

Negril still retains its laid-back roots.

Don't you wish you were there? – just a part of the giant Negril Beach

Dressing for dinner means popping a T-shirt over your swimsuit. By day everyone sunbathes, with breaks for snorkeling, jetskiing, or a parasail ride. The evening ritual is to gather with rum punch in hand to watch the sun slide from view into a molten sea below a sky of flaming orange and plum purple. After sunset Negril comes to life with pounding discos and live reggae concerts.

A virtually ruler-straight road, Norman Manley Boulevard runs the length of Long Bay. South of the tiny town center, West End Road meanders past a kaleidoscope of hotels, restaurants, and funky food stands that offer everything from magic mushroom omelettes to *nouvelle cuisine*. The entire West End sits atop dramatically sculpted cliffs that loom over the pellucid waters.

Negril's hustlers can be as annoying as flies. Their favorite sale item is *ganja* (marijuana) sold in joints the size of bazookas!

The Jamaica Tourist Board office (tel: (809) 957–4243) is in Plaza Adrija.

The Great Morass

This huge expanse of wetland pushes right up to the beach. Much of the 2-mile-wide swamp remains unexplored. It is a refuge for crocodiles, plus egrets, jacanas, and other rare birds.

The Negril River, which drains the swamps, is stained dark by peat deposits. Various earlier attempts to drain the swamps washed large amounts of silt out to sea, destroying a portion of the coral reef. Inevitably there is a fierce on-going battle between money-seeking developers and environmentalists.

The pirate "Calico" Jack Rackham (named for his penchant for calico underwear) was captured here in 1720 after lingering in the company of his amorous but no less bloodthirsty consorts, Anne Bonney and Mary Read. Rackham was strung from the gibbet at Port Royal; the female pirates "pleaded their stomachs, being quick with child" and were spared execution.

The islet offshore is Booby Cay, famous as a South Sea location in Walt Disney's *20,000 Leagues Under the Sea*. It is a nesting site for booby birds.

Bloody Bay

This scalloped bay, north of Long Bay, is the setting for three deluxe all-inclusive resorts. Where nudists now frolic whales were once beached and butchered.

The British Royal Navy considered the bay "conveniently situated for [its] men-of-war, during any rupture with Spain, to lie in wait for Spanish vessels passing to and fro from Havana." In 1702 a naval squadron under Admiral Benbow mustered here; another gathered in 1814 before bombarding New Orleans.

Negril Lighthouse

Negril's only historical structure is the lighthouse, which celebrated its centenary in 1994. Located at 18° 15' north by 78° 23' west, it marks the most westerly point of Jamaica, 3 miles south of the town.

It is possible to climb the 103 stairs by arrangement with the keeper. Among other sights are the original kerosene lamps. Today the 66-feet-tall lighthouse gives warning with an automatic, solar-powered light.

THE WHITE WITCH OF ROSE HALL

The sordid saga of the White Witch of Rose Hall is more fictional than factual; but it is an exhilarating tale nonetheless!

The legend tells of Annie Palmer, the wicked mistress who ruled over Rose Hall for 13 years. The epic of iniquity begins in 1820, when estate owner John Rose Palmer married his 18-year-old Irish bride, Anne May Patterson. Said to have been trained in voodoo by a Haitian priestess, Rose Hall's new mistress was as sadistic and sinful as she was petite and pretty. She supposedly tortured her slaves and lured into bed any man, black or white, whom she fancied.

According to a late Victorian version of the tale, she "poisoned her first husband, aided by her paramour, a Negro, whom she flogged to death to close his lips; again married, poisoned her second husband, whose death she hastened by stabbing him with a knife; married her second paramour . . . who disappeared mysteriously . . ."

Her fourth husband wisely abandoned her, leaving the lascivious Anne to the company of her slaves. Her orgy of dissipation ended one morning in 1833 when a slave lover strangled

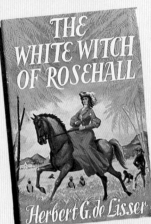

THE WHITE WITCH OF ROSEHALL
Herbert G. de Lisser

her in her bed at the Great House.

The tale is apocryphal. It is based on the fact that Rose Palmer, the first mistress of Rose Hall, indeed had four husbands. She died at the age of 72 in the 23rd year of her marriage to John Palmer, founder of Rose Hall. Research proves that the real Anne was also a model wife to John Rose Palmer. She died peacefully at Bonavista near Montego Bay in 1846.

The kernel of the legend arose even while Anne Palmer was still alive. The Revd Hope Waddell, writing of the neighboring Palmer property of Palmyra, recorded having being shown "the iron collars and spikes used by a lady owner there for the necks of her slaves, and also the bed on which she was found dead one morning, having been strangled." In 1868 the editor of the *Falmouth Post* apparently had the notion of linking Waddell's story with memories of a much-married mistress and published a story in which Anne Palmer first appeared as an evil murderess.

The tale is marvellously told in the novel *The White Witch of Rosehall*, by

Herbert G. de Lisser, 1958.

The witch is still rumored to haunt the ghostly-grey Great House. On 13 Friday 1979 thousands of onlookers watched as a group of Jamaican and US psychics attempted to make contact with Anne Palmer. Bambos, a well-known local clairvoyant, claimed to have made contact with Anne's spirit, which guided him to a large termite's nest containing a brass urn and a voodoo doll representing the charred remains of Anne Palmer.

Rose Hall (18th-century) and Anne Palmer's bedroom

Hands-on: A streamer-tailed hummingbird takes a drink at Rocklands

ROARING RIVER

Strangely impressive, the aptly named Roaring River gushes from the ground to form the Blue Hole, a circular jade-colored pool good for swimming. Picnicking is also popular beneath the sago palms and silk-cotton trees.
At Shrewsbury Estate, 2 miles northeast of Petersfield.

ROCKLANDS BIRD FEEDING STATION

Birds can be relied upon to show up each afternoon at Rocklands, situated at almost 1,000 feet with a marvellous view over Montego Bay. The feeding station is owned and operated by Lisa Salmon, as it has been for over 30 years – her knowledge of bird life is legendary.

You can feed grassquits and saffron finches from your hands, and streamer-tailed hummingbirds will perch on your fingers to drink sugar-water from tiny bottles.
Rocklands, Anchovy, St James (tel: (809) 952–2009). Open: daily, 3pm–dusk. Admission charge.

ROSE HALL

The most famous house in Jamaica, this grand 18th-century plantation house is perched atop a sweeping hillock carpeted in lime-green lawns. The hall's commanding presence is heightened by its thick granite walls. Inside is as cool as a well, and standing at the base of the sweeping staircase it is easy to imagine guests whirling around the high-ceilinged ballroom to a merry waltz while outside the slaves toiled beneath the evening sun.

The Georgian structure was built between 1770 and 1780 at the heyday of sugar. It fell into disuse at an early stage and was found in 1830 to be "unoccupied save by rats, bats, and owls." It remained an imposing ruin until 1966, when a wealthy American – John Rollins, former lieutenant-governor of Delaware – restored the house to haughty grandeur.

The ballroom retains the silk wall fabric – an exact reproduction of an original designed for Marie Antoinette. The house is fully furnished with original antiques, including Hepplewhite, Sheraton, and Chippendale furniture. Downstairs the dungeon has been turned into a pub straight out of *Treasure Island*.

The splendor of the Georgian house has long been overshadowed, however, by the legend of Anne Palmer, the White Witch of Rose Hall (see **The White Witch of Rose Hall**, page 106). In her bedroom is a plantation-made, Regency-style Jamaican mahogany bed in which she was supposedly entertained by her slave lovers.

Rose Hall, PO Box 186, Montego Bay (tel: (809) 953–2323). Open: daily, 9am–5:30pm. Tours every 15 minutes. 3 miles east of Montego Bay.

SAVANNA-LA-MAR

"Sav," as it is called locally, is a dilapidated port town and the capital of Westmoreland Parish. It was founded about 1703 at an unenviable location hemmed in by mangrove swamps. It has been destroyed several times by hurricanes.

In 1988 Hurricane Gilbert destroyed Sav's dock along with hundreds of old, poorly constructed wooden houses (most of which have been replaced by new, poorly constructed wooden houses). A few of the venerable timber houses with high-pitched shingled roofs remain.

Great George Street, the broad main street, stretches inland for over a mile. It terminates at the seaward end by the old fort, begun in 1755 and now swamped by sea water. More intriguing is the domed cast-iron fountain dating from 1887 opposite the courthouse.

18 miles east of Negril.

Intricate cast-iron fountain at Savanna-la-Mar (the name means "plain by the sea")

existence. The cottages are reminiscent of those in Germany's Weser valley, with a distinctive gable with two small windows above the doorway. Note the house just above the Catholic Church of the Sacred Heart, with false, painted doors, windows, and plants.

The church was established in 1873 by Father Tauer, who converted most residents to catholicism.

Seaford Town Historical Mini-Museum, in the church grounds, was founded in the 1970s by Father Francis Friesen.

24 miles south of Montego Bay. Museum open by request. Admission free, but a donation is appreciated.

SEAFORD TOWN

A curious anomaly, Seaford Town is home to a dwindling community of fair-skinned, blue-eyed farmers of German descent.

When slavery ended the Jamaican government encouraged European peasants to settle. Between 1834 and 1837 more than 1,000 immigrants came from North Germany; about 250 settled on Montpelier Mountain, site of today's Seaford (named after Lord Seaford, who donated the land). A newspaper of the time described Seaford as "a perfect sink-hole"; the domestic arrangements, complained the paper, were altogether un-English!

For 150 years the German stock has refused to integrate with black Jamaicans. They have retained their features by persistent in-breeding. Today only about 200 whites remain (many have emigrated to Canada in recent years), the German language has gone, and only a few scraps of German folklore endure.

Tiny houses of German provenance rise up the hillsides, from which the farmers eke out a none-too-profitable

SOLDIER STONE

This roadside marker at Struie was erected by members of the 6th Battalion Company (Light Infantry) in honor of Private Obediah Bell Chambers. According to the barely legible inscription Chambers was "cruelly butchered" when ambushed by rebellious slaves in January 1832. Local lore says that Chambers's stubborn mule refused to retreat with the rest of his company, and when his head was chopped off it fled and was found in Cuba.

The place is supposedly haunted. Listen for the clang of clashing swords at night!

5 miles west of Seaford Town; 21 miles south of Montego Bay.

TRYALL ESTATE

This former sugar plantation, 12 miles west of Montego Bay, is now a grand Jamaican resort with a mile-long beachfront and a spectacular

The Tryall Mill waterwheel dwarfs its attendant mechanic

1-800-238-5290

championship golf course (site of the Johnnie Walker Pro-Am Tournament).

The sugar estate was destroyed during the slave uprising of 1831–2, but the structures were rebuilt in 1834. The mill's old waterwheel still turns under the weight of water running down a 2-mile-long aqueduct from the Flint River.

The estate Great House is now the nucleus of the lobby and lounge of **Tryall Golf, Tennis and Beach Club** *(tel: (809) 956–5660)*. A gravestone embedded in the lawn in front of the entrance is that of the head driver of the estate who was "shot by the rebels while defending his master's property on the 8th of January 1832."

Note the cannons guarding the beach club.

Y S WATERFALLS

These triple-tiered cascades form a remote beauty spot reached by a 2-mile hike along a muddy jungle trail. Each fall shelters a limestone cave; each, too, tumbles into a pool good for swimming. Mosses and ferns thrive in the mists.

The enchanting Y S Waterfalls

The Y S cascades lie on a 2,000-acre working farm specializing in breeding tropical livestock. The land has belonged to the Browne family, descendants of the Marquis of Sligo, since 1887 (Sligo was governor of Jamaica in 1833, shortly before slavery was abolished). Near the bridge over the river you can explore the remains of the old sugar mill.

To visit it is necessary to book a tour through South Coast Safaris *(tel: (809) 965–2513)* or St Bess Attractions *(tel: (809) 965–2229)*.

The curious name derives from the Gaelic word "Wyess," meaning "winding," describing the course of the river. Wyess was abbreviated to Y S and adopted as the estate mark on barrels of sugar.

1 mile north of Middle Quarters; 35 miles west of Mandeville.

Montego Bay Walk

While Mo'Bay is renowned for its beaches, it also has plenty of historical edifices to enjoy. This walk through the heart of Jamaica's premier resort town leads past the most interesting and best-preserved buildings. It ends at Mo'Bay's famous crafts market. *Allow 2 hours.*

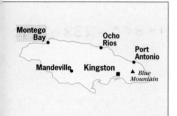

Begin at the old fort on Gloucester Avenue.

1 MONTEGO BAY FORT
This tiny fort still mounts a battery of George III cannons, now green with patina.

From the fort's upper reaches, stroll to the roundabout. Follow Fort Street as it swings south toward the town center.

2 SAM SHARPE SQUARE
This lively square centers on a traffic island with a fountain. It

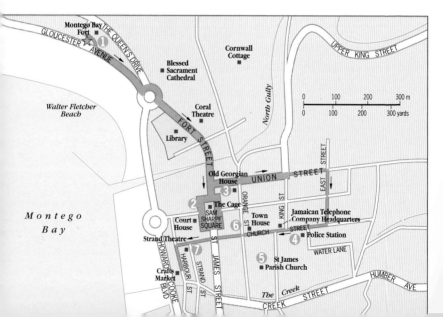

also holds The Cage, where runaway slaves and miscreants were imprisoned, and fine bronze statues of national heroes Paul Bogle and Sam Sharpe. On the south side are the ruins of the old courthouse.

Retrace your steps to Union Street. Turn right and walk 1 block.

3 GEORGIAN HOUSES
These two appealing 19th-century stone and brick buildings have been faithfully restored. One houses an art gallery, the other an up-scale restaurant. You can dine in the paved and shady courtyard *(tel: (809) 952–0632).*

Continue up Union Street to East Street. The "Slave Ring" that once stood on the northeastern corner was most likely used for cockfighting. Turn right. Turn right at Church Street.

4 CHURCH STREET
On the corner of Church Street and Water Lane is the police station, an octagonal, two-story plantation-style building with wide verandas supported by square, fluted columns. Opposite, on the corner of King Street, note the gleaming white Georgian structure with a doorway lit by brass lamps. On the junction's south side is another Georgian building – the towering, pink stucco headquarters of the Jamaican Telephone Company – with a soaring hardwood door.

Continue down Church Street.

5 ST JAMES PARISH CHURCH
The tall, handsome church of white limestone is in the shape of a Greek cross. It was restored after being wrecked by an earthquake in 1957. The churchyard

A shopkeeper hangs out her wares in a Montego Bay crafts market

contains interesting graves, many in a sorry state of dilapidation.

6 TOWN HOUSE
This stately red-brick mansion at 16 Church Street dates back to 1765 and now accommodates the popular Town House Restaurant *(tel: (809) 952-2660).*

Proceed down Church Street to Strand Street.

7 STRAND THEATRE
This 1950s, art-deco-style theater is now a cinema.

Walk 1 block down Church Street to Harbour Street. Cross the road and enter the crafts market. End your walk here.

Montego Bay Drive

A short jaunt into the rolling and rugged green hills leads to relatively isolated communities that retain remnants of their distinct culture. A working plantation and a bird sanctuary also lie tucked in the hills. The occasional sweeping vistas beg extra film! *Allow 4 hours, including stops.*

Depart Mo'Bay via Barnett Street (A1) westward to Reading. Turn left and follow the B8 uphill to Anchovy via a narrow limestone gorge. After 2 miles turn left for Rocklands Bird Feeding Station (the ½-mile climb is steep and potholed).

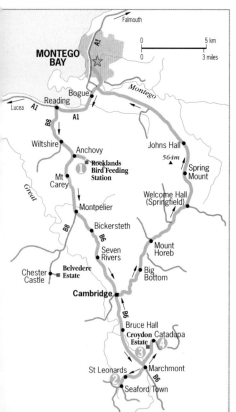

1 ROCKLANDS BIRD FEEDING STATION

A wide variety of birds, including the doctor bird, Jamaica's national bird, can be relied upon to show up mid-afternoons for feeding time. With luck you can have a hummingbird feed from your hand. *(tel: (809) 952-2009). Open: 2pm–dusk. Admission charge.*

Return to the B8. Turn left and continue south 3 miles to Montpelier. Turn left on to the B6 opposite the Texaco station (follow the sign to Croydon Estate). Beyond Cambridge are dramatic vistas of serrated mountains and deep-forested valleys. 10 miles beyond Montpelier turn right at the 4-way junction at Marchmont. 2 miles farther a sign reads: "Now Entering Seaford. A German Town Founded in 1835." Continue to the T-junction. Turn right for Seaford Town.

2 SEAFORD TOWN

This neat hillside settlement has gabled wooden houses reminiscent of cottages in Germany's Weser valley. One-third of

Known as Mo'Bay, lively Montego Bay is the best known of Jamaica's resorts

Seaford's inhabitants are of German stock: blond-haired, blue-eyed but inbred and dwindling. The Historical Museum next to the Sacred Heart Catholic Church illustrates the town's heritage *(drive to the Sacred Mission, for the key)*.

Return to Marchmont. Cross the junction and follow the road to the right towards Catadupa. Turn left at the sign for Croydon Estate.

3 CROYDON ESTATE
Croydon grows coffee, citrus, and pineapples on 132 acres of carefully tended terraces. A "see, hear, touch, and taste" tour includes a Jamaican lunch served atop a hill with a commanding view of the valley. *(tel: (809) 952–4137). Open: Tuesday, Wednesday, Friday, 10am–3pm. Admission charge.*

Return to the road to Catadupa; turn left into town. The road beyond Catadupa is suitable only for jeeps; as one local says, "Road bad to Hell, mon!"

4 CATADUPA
This erstwhile center of coffee-growing has gone into decline since the railway shut down in 1992. The station still stands, as does the factory for washing and pulping coffee beans.

Return to Marchmont and Cambridge. Turn right for Mount Horeb and Welcome Hall (locally called Springfield; the road is not signposted). The well-paved, lonesome road switchbacks through dramatic karst country of deep troughs and conical hillocks. Turn right 6 miles beyond Cambridge; then left, 3 miles farther, at Welcome Hall. Continue downhill to Montego Bay.

South Central

*T*he South Coast is a secret corner that stands on the verge of discovery. Unblemished as yet are its secluded beaches, hidden coves, soaring cliffs, charming fishing villages, and above all serene mountain scenery.

Civic leaders are working heartily to promote the South Coast as a tourist destination. The region offers a contrast to the traditional sun-and-sand vacation. A new concept of community-based tourism has been launched in Mandeville, and the Sandals chain is spearheading shoreline development with an all-inclusive resort – the South Coast's first.

The South Coast is basically a great basin rimmed by mountains. The flat fertile plain and verdant highland valleys constitute the "breadbasket of Jamaica." The geographic contrasts, however, are startling. To the west the waters of the Black River gather in great swamps, the largest wetlands area in the Caribbean, known as the Great Morass. Guided tours take you into a realm known for its rich bird life and crocodiles. Here, too, shading the A2, is Bamboo Avenue, a

SOUTH CENTRAL JAMAICA

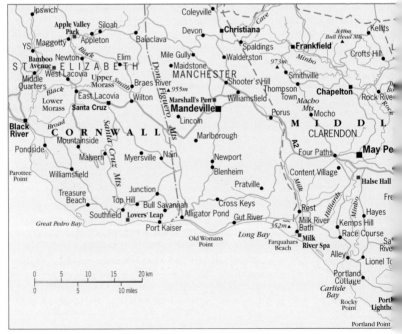

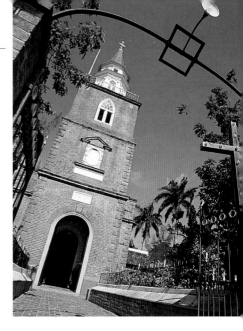

Cathedral of St Jago de la Vega

2-mile glade of giant bamboos over a century old and the gateway to the west.

Following the A2 east you snake until eventually you arrive on a plateau hidden away in the Don Figuero Mountains. At its center sits Mandeville, which British residents made their own. It retains a dash of old England. Farther south lies sleepy Malvern, a refreshingly cool hilltop treasure that has been left to Jamaicans.

Here, 2,000 feet up in the mountains where the air is redolent with night-blooming jasmine, the roads that cut through the Mocho, Don Figuero, and Santa Cruz Mountains rise, dip, and curve through very untropical terrain.

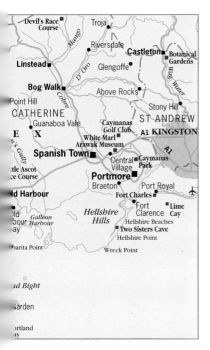

Tourists may also be surprised to find themselves surrounded by cactus and parched semisavanna. There *is* water here. To sample it, visit Milk River Spa, where the mineral springs are more potent than any in Europe. The waters must be healthy, for rare manatees and crocodiles survive amid the coastal estuaries.

Farther east lies Spanish Town, fascinating for history buffs. The Spanish, the English, and the African all left their mark on Jamaica's erstwhile capital city. Sadly Hurricane Gilbert dealt the town a devastating blow in 1988. The Cathedral Church of St James, however, has lost none of its stunning if simple glory.

Fishing is a staple of the south coast. Beaches are highlighted by Treasure Beach, anchored by one of the quaintest and quietest fishing villages of all. The awesome cliffs at Lovers' Leap are nearby.

The stock of hotel rooms is small, with none of the impersonal high-rises of the major resort centers. Choose a cosy inn by a lonesome beach – you can walk for miles without ever seeing a soul!

Mandeville

*M*andeville, capital of Manchester Parish, is named after Lord Mandeville, whose father, the Duke of Manchester, was governor of Jamaica in the early 1800s. The town is perched at a crisp 2,000-foot elevation. Established in 1816, it served for much of the century as a hill station for British regiments.

Mandeville has long been favored by expatriates for its year-round spring-like climate. A century ago anyone who was anyone vacationed here. Later it became a retirement haven for English folk who found that it reminded them of home.

Echoes of England are everywhere. Quaint Georgian buildings surround Jamaica's only village "green." Dry-stone walls line the narrow streets, and many locals take pride in nursing their English-style gardens. The discovery of bauxite in the 1950s fostered the influx of a new breed of expatriate – North Americans.

Today Mandeville (pop. 35,000) is the fifth-largest town in Jamaica. It is an agricultural center and dormitory town for two alumina companies that have laid out expansive residential areas.

Mandeville, 61 miles west of Kingston, is surrounded by hills reminiscent of England and vales laid out for citrus production (particularly the ortanique, a locally developed hybrid, part orange, part tangarine, and totally unique).

The courthouse at Mandeville was built from limestone blocks by slaves

Bill Laurie's Steak House
This popular restaurant offers a bird's-

eye view of Mandeville. The restaurant, housed in old Bloomfield Great House, has a display of antique cars and license plates.
Bloomfield Gardens (tel: (809) 962–3116).

Cecil Charlton Park
Mandeville's lively town square, locally called "The Green," was recently renamed Cecil Charlton Park after the former mayor (see **Mr Charlton's Mansion**).

Dominating the square is the Parish Church of St Mark, built of limestone, and, opposite, the Georgian courthouse, with an attractive horseshoe staircase and a portico on Doric columns. Both date from 1820. The old rectory, next to the courthouse, is Mandeville's oldest structure.

To the east is the Mandeville Hotel. This former army officer's quarters dates from 1875 and claims to be the oldest hotel in Jamaica.

Kirkvine Works
Kirkvine Works, northeast of town, was opened in 1952 as Jamaica's first alumina plant – it remains the island's largest. The owner, Alcan Jamaica Co., welcomes visitors with 1 day's notice *(tel: (809) 962–3141)*. Their massive landholdings – 31,000 acres under rehabilitation or not yet mined – are given over to livestock and citrus.

Mr Charlton's Mansion
The strange pagoda-like mansion crowning Huntingdon Summit, 3 miles south of the town, is the ostentatious home of Cecil C Charlton, millionaire politician, farmer, and Mayor of Mandeville for over 20 years until 1986.

A highlight is an indoor pond connected to an outdoor swimming pool

St Mark's, "The Green," Mandeville

by an underground tunnel.
Call ahead for an appointment (tel: (809) 962–2274). Open: daily, except Wednesday and Saturday. Free, but a donation to a local charity is welcome.

Pickapeppa Factory
The Pickapeppa Factory makes the famous sinus-searing gourmet sauce, conjured from a closely guarded recipe using tropical fruits and spices.
Tel: (809) 962–2928. Tours by appointment. Located at the junction of the B4, B5, and B6.

Williamsfield Great House
In 1770 Captain George Heron built Williamsfield Great House on 10,000 acres of land granted to his great-grandfather, who landed with the 1655 expedition that captured Jamaica from the Spanish. Heron built four Great Houses in Jamaica and maintained separate families in each. It has been beautifully restored.
Williamsfield, 5 miles northwest of Mandeville. Tours available by request (tel: (809) 963–4214).

ALLIGATOR POND

Dugout canoes still line the beach at this fishing village, 20 miles south of Mandeville. The early-morning fish market adds additional color. Hungry? Take your pick of stands selling bammy, fresh fish, and lobster. A local fisher will happily take you out fishing for a fee.

The coastal estuaries are lined by mangrove swamps, a habitat of manatees, or sea cows, the gentle and sluggish marine mammals that gave rise during Columbus's time to the legend of mermaids. Numerous during Arawak times, the harmless creatures, which grow to 14 feet, have since been decimated for their hide, meat, and blubber.

Alligator Hole is a wildlife preserve popular with waterfowl. Here a freshwater river emerges from a small cave. The refreshingly cool water is reportedly good for swimming. The nibbling you feel is only a toothy though retiring crocodile (locally called alligators).

A fisher shows off some of his catch at Alligator Pond

BAMBOO AVENUE

Hurricane Gilbert almost tore down this glade of frilly bamboos that arch over the road. The 2-mile-long sun-dappled nave is almost fully recovered and now over a century old. The grove, a well-known landmark between Middle Quarters and Lacovia, is maintained by staff from the Hope Botanical Gardens. It is extremely photogenic and well worth the drive.

CHRISTIANA

This small market town is surrounded by lush agricultural land cultivated by light-skinned farmers of German provenance, the offspring of mercenaries who received land grants in Jamaica after fighting for England during the American War of Independence. The main crop is Irish potatoes.

Note the imposing police station and courthouse, dating from 1896, and the intriguing Moravian church, built about 1891.
10 miles north of Mandeville.

COLBECK CASTLE

The ruined "castle," 2 miles northwest of Old Harbour, was built in the late 18th century and named after – though apparently not built by – Colonel John Colbeck, an early English settler. The great grey-brick mansion is now but a shell surrounded by tobacco fields. Notice the underground slave quarters at each corner.

GREAT MORASS (UPPER AND LOWER)

This vast area of rushes, reeds, mangroves, and other rare wetland

Bamboo Avenue: badly damaged by the hurricane in 1988, but it soon grew back

species suits its name – a watery swamp fed by the Black River and its many tributaries. The Morass forms a rare remnant habitat for fish, especially tarpon and snook, and birds such as egrets, jacanas, and even ospreys. It is also Jamaica's major refuge for "alligators" (American crocodiles), which sun themselves on the muddy riverbanks.

Various schemes to drain and develop the swamps date back to 1738 when the British attempted to settle some loyalist refugees from Carolina, but local opposition to the scheme led to its failure. Even today the locals make great play of the fact that even a settler whose name was Frogge found the area too damp. In the 1970s and 1980s an attempt was made to develop the land for rice, but this also failed.

Locals have found success in growing ganja (marijuana), and a company called Jamculture raises shrimp and fish.

(See also **Getting Away From it All**).

HALSE HALL

Splendidly situated amid a rolling plantation, Halse Hall is one of the oldest continuously occupied Great Houses in Jamaica. The pretty stone-and-wood structure was built as a fortified home by a British soldier, Thomas Halse. Beneath lies a Spanish foundation that dates back to when the property was originally known as Hato de Bueno Vista (Ranch of the Beautiful View). It was recently restored and is furnished with period pieces.
Tour by prior permission (tel: (809) 986–2215). 3 miles south of May Pen, on the road to Lionel Town. Admission charge.

HELLSHIRE BEACHES

This paternoster string of white-sand beaches fringes a barren promontory southwest of Kingston. The talcum-fine beaches remain virtually unknown to tourists. There are few facilities away from the two most popular beaches, Fort Clarence and Naggo Head. Plan accordingly.

Rough, unmarked trails lead from cove to cove. Bird-watchers should take their binoculars for spotting rare shore birds that play tag with the waves.
14 miles southwest of Kingston. Admission free.

Fort Clarence Beach

A day here is a sociology lesson in Jamaican ways. The resort gets crowded on weekends with congenial Kingstonians who flock for family barbecues, soccer games, and general play. Body-beautiful contests and reggae concerts are regularly held here.

The water is ideal for swimming. There are changing facilities, security patrols, and food shacks selling the local speciality, "fish and festival" – fried fish with sweet dumpling.

The name derives from a small fort on the headland.

Naggo Head Beach

Naggo Head Beach, north of Fort Clarence, is even trendier. Salt Pond, nearby, was once a fishing ground of Arawak Indians; abundant fish still provide food for a family of crocodiles. Swimming is not recommended!

HELLSHIRE HILLS

These limestone hills backing the Hellshire Beaches lure hikers and nature lovers. The porous bedrock, called honeycomb, soaks up the little rain it

receives; the surface soil is therefore quite thin and hospitable only to cactus and thorny shrub.

Trails lead through the dry tropical deciduous forest and spiny scrubland that form the heart of a nature reserve. Iguanas, rare elsewhere, are commonly seen. The hills' unique wildlife includes the endangered Jamaican coney, a nocturnal mammal often called the Jamaican rabbit. To the southeast mangrove swamps are inhabited by manatees.

Caves pock the landscape, one of which – Two Sisters Cave – is a tourist attraction. Rock-carved steps lead you down to a pool where river bass thrive. From the observation platform you can look across the shimmering waters to a rock-carving left by Arawak Indians.

Urbanization is fast encroaching. Portmore is the most developed of a series of dormitory communities being developed as suburbs of Kingston.

LACOVIA

Lacovia, immediately east of Bamboo Avenue, is a one-street village (the longest on the island) that sprawls along the A2 and is divided into West Lacovia, East Lacovia, and Lacovia Tombstone. The English and Spanish fought a battle for the ford over the Black River in 1655.

In 1723 Lacovia was named the capital of St Elizabeth but lost its title after a long dispute with Black River, the courts and other functions being alternated between the two towns for half a century. Several tombstones attest that Lacovia was at that time mostly inhabited by Jews. It grew to be an important river port from which logwood and fustic (both used to extract dyes) were shipped.

On the road in front of the Texaco station are two tombstones containing the remains of two soldiers who killed each other in a duel in 1738.

LOVERS' LEAP

Not for the faint-hearted! Here the Santa Cruz Mountains shoulder right up to the coast, and a 1,700-foot cliff plunges sheer to the ocean. Far below waves crash ashore on the jagged rocks.

Climb the steps to the right of the unfinished restaurant for spectacular views along the coast. From on high, the blue Caribbean stretches as far as the eye can see. You can make eye-to-eye contact with buzzards – John Crows – that soar on the thermals.

According to legend, the spot is named after two lovers – slaves –who had been forbidden to meet, by their respective owners. The illicit lovers met anyway and, when about to be captured here, leapt to their deaths rather than be split apart.

Adjacent is a red-and-white-hooped lighthouse whose grounds contain a military radar used to track drug trafficking.

Lovers' Leap – a view to a death if the legend is to be believed

MALVERN

Off the tourist path but well worth seeking out, Malvern straddles the Santa Cruz mountains 2,400 feet up, 11 miles south of Santa Cruz. Its crisp setting is extremely picturesque.

It was once a resort town popular with the well-to-do. Today Malvern is a prosperous agricultural community with several intriguing old stone buildings. Look for Deep Dene, on the road to Black River. It has a steep, sloping roof and low veranda fringed with gingerbread trim – the essence of picture-postcard pretty. Deep Dene is one of three acclaimed and historic schools, another being the Bethlehem Teacher Training College.

The mountain roads that lead to Malvern offer spectacular vistas down over the bright-green plains, and occasional peeks across the deep valley towards Mandeville.

MARSHALL'S PEN

At the heart of this 300-acre cattle farm, one of the most acclaimed cattle-rearing centers in the Caribbean, is a well-kept

18th-century Great House that once belonged to the Earl of Balcarres, Governor of Jamaica (1795–1801). The home, off Winston Jones Highway north of Mandeville, is filled with antique treasures, as well as a stamp and shell collection. Beyond the beautiful garden is a bird sanctuary and nature reserve replete with reptiles, butterflies, and other insects.

Overnight stays can be arranged through the owners, Robert and Anne Sutton. Mr Sutton, an ornithologist and descendant of one of the earliest British settlers, leads birding trips along the nature trails.

Marshall's Pen, PO Box 58, Mandeville (tel: (809) 962–2260). Open: daily, by appointment. Admission charge.

MAY PEN

This market town midway between Mandeville and Spanish Town lies at the heart of a highly developed agricultural district. Stop in on Friday or Saturday for the lively market. The annual Denbigh Show, Jamaica's major agricultural show, is held here in the first week of August.

An American air base was established nearby at Vernham Field during World War II. Today it is used for occasional auto-racing and illegal marijuana trafficking – not a place to drop in casually!

MILK RIVER BATH

If Jamaica's warm seas do not relax you, head for Milk River Bath, Jamaica's foremost spa. The hot waters that emerge from the base of the Carpenter Mountains are the most radioactive waters on earth – three times more so

Old World courtesy: Mr Sutton in his lovely home, Marshall's Pen

Milk River Bath's spa waters are said to have great healing qualities

than those of Karlovy Vary in the Czech Republic, and nine times that of Bath in England.

An immersion is supposed to cure rheumatism, eczema, sciatica, lumbago, gout, and a host of other complaints. The recommended treatment is three soaks per day, each no longer than 20 minutes. A large swig of murky water is part of the cure (presumably, a good way to increase your half-life!). "Overwhelming vitality is restored," claims the homey Milk River Bath Hotel *(tel: (809) 924-9544)*.

The water's miraculous properties

were discovered by a slave who had been lashed and left for dead. When he reappeared, miraculously healed, estate owner Jonathan Ludford built the first baths in 1794.

Milk River is popular on weekends with Kingstonians. Take your pick between the rather dingy hotel spa, where massages are also available, or a public spa and swimming pool nearby *(open: weekends and public holidays, 10am–6pm)*.

The primitive road continues past tall cacti to a quaint fishing village where the river meets Farquhars Beach. The mangrove swamps here harbor American crocodiles ("alligators"). You can watch fishers bringing in their catch and enjoy a simple meal in one of the rustic restaurants run by Rastas.
28 miles southeast of Mandeville.

OLD HARBOUR

Old Harbour, on the A2 midway between May Pen and Spanish Town, is a sleepy market town with a strong fishing tradition. At its heart is an elegant iron Victorian clock tower topped by a filigree crown. It is so superbly maintained that you can set your watch by its time.

Classical grandeur in Spanish Town: the white-stucco Rodney Memorial building

SPANISH TOWN

Jamaica's third-largest town, 14 miles west of Kingston, is the cradle of the island's modern history. The Spanish established their capital here in 1523, centerd on a plaza – today's Parade. When the British captured the city in 1655 Cromwell's soldiers razed the Spanish buildings, which were gradually replaced with structures of surprising elegance. The town remained Jamaica's capital until 1872.

The Parade is surrounded by decrepit Georgian buildings; the garden shaded by tall palms was ravaged by Hurricane Gilbert and also has gone to ruin.

Of note are the colorful market; King Street, with Georgian houses with jalousies and "coolers"; a venerable though neglected military barracks dating to 1791; and an iron bridge over the Rio Cobre, shipped from England in 1801 and the oldest surviving cast-iron bridge in the Americas.

Rodney Memorial

This noble edifice on the north side of the Parade celebrates Admiral Rodney's victory over a French and Spanish invasion fleet in April 1782. A marble statue of Rodney dressed in a Roman toga is enclosed by a cupola'd "temple." Relief panels on the pediment depict the battle. Two brass cannons from the French flagship flank the statue (by eminent English artist John Bacon).

Behind the memorial are the Archives Office and Records Office housing important historical and legal documents.

The empty red-brick shell opposite was once the courthouse, built in 1819 but destroyed by fire in 1986.

Old Kings House

An impressive porticoed Georgian façade is all that remains of the once-magnificent red-brick structure built in 1762 as the official residence of the governors of Jamaica. It, too, was destroyed by fire, in 1925.

Opposite, on the east side, is the former House of Assembly, built in 1760. The impressive brick building with pillared wooden balcony overhanging a shady colonnade now houses the offices of the St Catherine Parish Council.

People's Museum of Craft and Technology

The museum, operated by the Institute of Jamaica, is housed in the old stables of Old Kings House. It provides an intriguing entrée to early Jamaican culture.

There are reconstructions of a smithy, or farrier's, tools, plus early carpenters' tools, Indian corn grinders and cassava press, pottery, baskets, and so on, and a model of the original Old Kings House. The grounds contain an old sugar press, coffee huskers, corn grinders, and dilapidated old carriages.

There is also a restaurant and bar.
Open: weekdays, 10am–4pm. Admission charge.

Cathedral of St Jago de la Vega

One of the prettiest churches in Jamaica, the red-brick cathedral is topped by an octagonal steeple with Corinthian columns. The church dates from 1714. It was built on the site of a 1523 Spanish church, the first cathedral in the New World. The original black-and-white checkered floor is studded with graves dating to 1662.

The beautiful interior features wooden fluted pillars, carved pews and choir stalls, a beamed ceiling, stained glass, and a large organ from 1849.

TREASURE BEACH

If there is treasure to be found in Jamaica it lies on the south coast at Treasure Beach, a seemingly endless crescent of coral-colored sand. There are several places to stay, including the marvellously positioned Treasure Beach Hotel *(tel: (809) 965–0110)*.

The fishing pirogues at the eastern end are worked by blue-eyed descendants of Scottish seamen shipwrecked in the 19th century.
19 miles southeast of Black River.

WHITE MARL ARAWAK MUSEUM

Worth a peek, the Arawak Museum houses a major collection of Arawak Indian finds. It is sited on the largest Amerindian settlement in Jamaica and includes middens, a reconstruction of an Arawak village, plus comprehensive displays that tell of the social and economic life of the Arawaks.
Open: weekdays, 10am–4pm. Admission charge. Off the Nelson Mandela Freeway, 2 miles east of Spanish Town.

Vegetation festoons the old iron bridge across the Rio Cobre at Spanish Town

Mandeville Drive

This country drive leads into the heart of some of Jamaica's prettiest scenery. Parts are reminiscent of England, with lime-green meadows lined by limestone walls and sheep and cattle grazing the margins on each side. Elsewhere are sugarcane fields, flat and green as a billiard table, backed by the forest-clad conical hills of the Cockpit Country, traditionally one of the most inaccessible and remote areas of the island. Even today roads are few and little-used. *Allow 4–5 hours, including stops.*

From Mandeville, the center of a rural and recently industrialized area built in the style of an English country town, follow New Green Road north to Mark Post. Turn left onto the B6 1 mile beyond Martin's Hill Orchid Sanctuary. Continue for 4 miles. Turn left at the sign for Comfort Hall. Follow the sign for Balaclava; then turn right at mile 13 and again about 4 miles farther. The road winds through a broad valley and Siloah, a charming village of old wooden houses. Beyond Siloah, the Appleton Rum Factory is on your right.

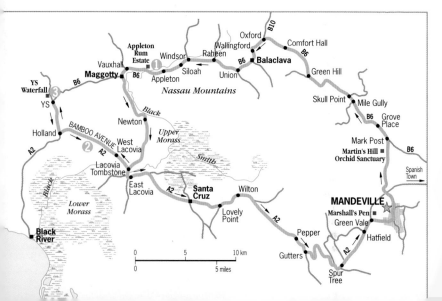

1 APPLETON RUM ESTATE

The Appleton estate has been growing sugarcane and turning it into rum since 1749. The Appleton Estate Rum Tour provides an inside look at the distillery and the distilling process. Newly cut cane can be seen being transported by JCBs and then rolled through giant crushers to release the juice. After being boiled at very high temperatures, the juice is crystallized into sugar using massive centrifuges. While here visitors can taste the fresh-pressed cane juice and molasses, as well as savor the famous rums. There is a restaurant and bar on the site.

Continue west for ½ mile to a roundabout. Here turn left for Maggotty; then follow the road south to Lacovia Tombstone, where a tombstone beside the gas station commemorates an English soldier, Thomas Jordan Spencer, an ancestor of both Winston Churchill and Princess Diana. Turn right onto the A2 and follow the road west for 2 miles to reach Bamboo Avenue.

2 BAMBOO AVENUE

An extremely photogenic, 2-mile-long glade of bushy bamboos that curve over to form a cool, green tunnel. The giant bamboos date back to the 19th century. Fields of citrus fruit and sugarcane lie on either side of the road.

About 1 mile west of Bamboo Avenue turn right at Holland onto a dirt road leading to Y S. The ruler-straight track leads past a papaya plantation and meadows grazed by Red Poll cattle.

3 Y S WATERFALL

Y S Falls in St Elizabeth Parish is one of Jamaica's largest, most scenic and least

The Appleton estate rum distillery is both the oldest and the biggest in Jamaica

known cataracts. The cascade descends 120 feet like a staircase, with cool pools for swimming. The falls are actually on private property, but access to them can be arranged in advance by calling St Bess Attractions *(tel: (809) 965–2229)* or South Coast Safaris *(tel: (809) 965–2513)*.

Retrace your route back to the A2, which will take you back to Mandeville.

PIRATES

Pirates fill the most violent chapter in Jamaica's chromatic history. For almost a century these wild and ruthless sea rovers raped, pillaged, and plundered their way around the Caribbean.

They began life in the mid-1600s as "buccaneers" (after the boucan, a wooden rack used to dry hides and meat), a band of sedentary misfits who congregated on Tortuga, off Hispaniola.

When the Spaniards drove them out they washed ashore in Jamaica,

Captain Kidd buries his treasure – but will he remember the spot?

formed the Confederacy of the Brethren of the Coast, and turned to ruthless plunder. Success soon swelled their numbers and fostered the rise of Port Royal as their base.

Nourished by booty, Port Royal rapidly evolved (or degenerated) into a hive of debauchery known as the "wickedest city in the world." John Esquemeling, himself a buccaneer, wrote that he saw one fellow "give unto a common strumpet five hundred pieces-of-eight only that he might see her naked."

When the Second Dutch War began in 1665 the English legalized the buccaneers as "privateers" to harass Spanish and Dutch shipping. The pirates reached their zenith under Henry Morgan, a rapacious Welsh sea captain who led a ruinous rape of the Spanish Main, crowned by the sacking and destruction of Panama in 1671.

Eventually Morgan was knighted, named Jamaica's lieutenant-governor, and charged with suppressing the buccaneers. Though Port Royal was destroyed by an earthquake in 1692, pirates multiplied. Their voracity and sadism increased in proportion. No vessel, town, or plantation was safe.

This era of infamy bred such colorful figures as Blackbeard (Edwin Teach), who carried lighted fuses in his beard, and Calico Jack (Jack Rackham), so called because of his penchant for calico underwear. In 1718 Blackbeard was captured, and his head was hung from the mainmast of his ship; Rackham was captured and executed in 1720, and his body was left to rot in an iron cage near Port Royal.

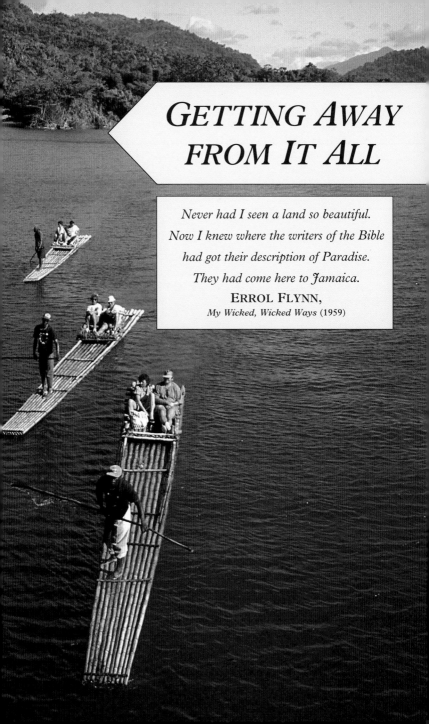

GETTING AWAY FROM IT ALL

Never had I seen a land so beautiful.
Now I knew where the writers of the Bible
had got their description of Paradise.
They had come here to Jamaica.

ERROL FLYNN,
My Wicked, Wicked Ways (1959)

APPLETON RUM ESTATE TOUR

Tasteful describes this ½-day excursion by tour bus. After skirting the wild Cockpit Country you arrive at the Appleton Rum Estate and distillery, set alongside the Black River in a lovely green valley surrounded by sugarcane fields and mountains. Here a tour reveals the secrets behind Jamaica's most potent elixir.

Inside the distillery visitors get to sample freshly pressed cane juice as well as molasses, "wet sugar," "high wine," and flavorful rum, which has been blended here since 1749.

The tour includes hotel transfers in Montego Bay, plus picnic lunch and complimentary rum punch in an air-conditioned lounge.

Jamaica Estate Tours Ltd, c/o Appleton Estate, Siloah, St Elizabeth (tel: (809) 963–2210 or (809) 997–6077). Admission charge.

BEACH PARTIES

Let your hair down by day at a daytime "boonoonoonoos" (beach party) that guarantees you rum-assisted fun in the sun. Most include exclusive use of the beach, free hotel pickup and return, open bar, water sports, entertainment (usually a reggae band), and barbecue lunch.

Rose Hall *(PO Box 186, Montego Bay (tel: (809) 953–2323)* offers a "five-Star Tour" that combines a fascinating tour of the historic Great House with a private beach party and Jamaican barbecue.

The ½-day **Miskito Cove Beach Picnic** *(tel: (809) 952–5164)* includes jet-ski rides, snorkeling, a glass-bottomed boat ride, windsurfing, sailing, and a bamboo raft ride. It takes place at Bamboo Bay, adjacent to Lucea harbor,

25 miles west of Montego Bay. Similar is the **Tropical Beach Club** *(tel: (809) 952–3000),* which features a protected reef for snorkeling, plus a special health spa, beauty salon, steam room, and masseuse – for those who tire of volleyball and limbo on the beach.

In Negril **Aqua Nova Water Sports** hosts a 3-hour cruise party. A 45-foot trimaran whisks passengers to Booby Cay for an "Island Picnic" and clothes-optional sunning. For information contact *Negril Beach Club, PO Box 7, Negril (tel: (809) 957-4221).*

BLUE MOUNTAIN DOWNHILL BICYCLE TOUR

This full-day tour starts 5,060 feet up in the mountains and, as advertised, is all downhill. Hence no pedalling! The exhilarating descent leads through lush rainforest, past coffee plantations, and over rickety bridges. It includes lunch, plus a stop to sample delectable Blue Mountain coffee fresh from the grinders and roasters.

*For information contact **Blue Mountain Tours Ltd**, 152 Main Street, Ocho Rios (tel: (809) 974–0635) or PO Box 84, Port Antonio (tel: (809) 993–2242).*

The **Jamaica Alternative Tourism, Camping and Hiking Association** (JATCHA) *(PO Box 216, Kingston 7 (tel: (809) 927–2097))* also arranges bike trips.

COFFEE FACTORY TOURS

Stop in at a coffee plantation for a pick-me-up. Jamaica's exalted Blue Mountain coffee (see pages 46–7) is grown, processed, and milled at the **Mavis Bank (Central) Coffee Factory** in Mavis Bank. A tour concludes in the tasting room where a professional taster will teach you the etiquette of appreciation. After sampling the aromatic roasts you

This guide will cheerfully show you around Mavis Bank Coffee Factory

are sure to pull out your wallet. Coffee direct from the factory sells for about one-fifth the price in the UK or the USA. *Tours by appointment (tel: (809) 924-9503).*

En route stop in at **World's End** where delicious "Old Jamaica" coffee liqueurs are conjured up in a small factory that clings to the mountainside. *Tours by appointment (tel: (809) 927-1943).*

In the central highlands follow your nose to the **High Mountain Coffee Factory** *(tel: (809) 963-4211)* at Williamsfield, near Mandeville. The factory specializes in High Mountain coffee, a lighter, sweeter brew than Blue Mountain. *Tours by appointment only.* Also in Williamsfield is the **Pioneer Chocolate Factory** *(tel: (809) 963-4216)*, where you may sample chocolate made from locally produced cocoa.

COMMUNITY TOURISM

Seeking an alternative to a sun-and-sand vacation? **Country Styles Ltd** *(PO Box 60, Mandeville; tel: (809) 962–3725)*, offers vacation experiences aimed at sponsoring development among communities traditionally bypassed by the tourist market. Visits with local families and accommodations in rural homes introduce you to Jamaican community life and culture. *For further information contact the Visitor Information Centre at the Astra Country Inn, 62 Ward Avenue, Mandeville (tel: (809) 962–3265).*

CRYSTAL SPRING GARDENS

This 158-acre tropical theme park/bird sanctuary/botanical garden delights visitors with 15,000 varieties of plants, including a stunning array of orchids. Hummingbirds are everywhere. A well-stocked pond caters to fishing. The less sedentary can go clip-clopping on horseback through the semiwild estate or canoe across the lagoon while the less

active relax under shady guava groves. Camping is allowed.

The old sugar property has a small museum and waterwheel. It was here in the last century that nine mongooses were introduced to control rats; their progeny have decimated indigenous wildlife and domestic chickens. *Tel: (809) 996–2020. Open: daily, 9am–6pm. Admission charge. 2 miles east of Buff Bay.*

CUBA

Europeans and Canadians have fallen in love with Cuba's silky sands, satin waters, and trove of colonial treasures. Several Jamaican companies offer tours to Havana, Santiago, or Varadero, a 12-mile-long finger of land with powder-white beaches that outdo even Negril's.

Sunholiday Travel *(tel: (809) 979–6672)* will whisk you to Santiago for a day, with a tour of the Moncada Barracks, Morro Castle, and Bacardi factory. Santiago is Cuba's most historic city and the center of the resistance movements that culminated in the 1959 Revolution.

Caribic Ltd *(69 Gloucester Ave, Montego Bay; tel: (809) 979-0322)* offers two exciting nights in Havana, the Cuban capital and the "Paris of the Caribbean." Its narrow, cobblestoned streets brim with baroque and neo-classical cathedrals, palaces, museums, and wide, palm-lined boulevards.

You can even cruise to Santiago for the weekend aboard the *Caribbean Queen*, a three-deck cruiser that sails from Port Antonio and Ocho Rios on Monday and Thursday. *For further information contact **InterCaribe Tours**,*

These superb orchids are just some of many at Crystal Spring Gardens

All aboard for the Black River Safari – but watch out for the crocodiles!

11 1/2 Ardenne Road, Kingston 10.

Your passport is required – it will *not* be stamped by the Cuban authorities.

ECO-TOURS

Eco-tourism – travel that contributes to the conservation of natural environments – is growing in popularity in Jamaica.

The 2-hour **Black River Safari** explores the Upper and Lower Morass, the biggest and most diverse swamp system in the Caribbean. Ten- and twenty-five-seater motor launches leave the town of Black River for a 7-mile guided tour through a region that resembles the Florida Everglades. Over 100 species of birds roost here, including herons, ospreys, chocolate-hued jacanas, and egrets. With luck you may see freshwater turtles and crocodiles eyeing you leerily, as well as shrimp fishers plying their trade in dugout canoes hung with shrimp pots. Colorful water lilies and delicate hyacinths grow in abundance.
*For further information contact **South Coast Safaris**, 1 Crane Road, Black River, or PO Box 129, Mandeville (tel: (809) 965–2513).*

In Port Royal **Morgan's Harbour Hotel and Marina** *(tel: (809) 924–8464)* offers dolphin- and bird-viewing trips to the mangrove-covered cays that border the alluvial strip and natural breakwater that separates Kingston Harbour from the sea. The cays shelter natural oyster beds, crocodiles, and pelican and frigate bird colonies that can be approached for close-up views of nesting birds. Dolphins have recently returned to the harbor and regularly play around the boats.

HELITOURS

If you think Jamaica looks fabulous on the ground, wait till you see it from the air. Have a bird's-eye adventure made easy, albeit at a sky-high price, through **Helitours Ltd** *(tel: (809) 979–8290)*. Opt for a 15-minute "fun hop" over Montego Bay; a 1-hour "Jamaica showcase"; or a day-long "island delight" that includes stops for tours and meals in Port Antonio, Kingston, and Negril.

Your lofty perch is a four-passenger Bell 206B Jetranger III. The service operates from Ocho Rios and Montego Bay.

Many campers and hikers heading for the Blue Mountains (right) start from the Maya Lodge and Hiking Centre in Kingston

HIKING

Jamaica is laced with thousands of miles of trails that serve both locals and adventurous Indiana Joneses.

The best hiking is in the Blue Mountains, where trails are categorized as guided, nonguided, or wilderness. Streams and waterfalls are abundant, as is wildlife rarely seen elsewhere on the island. Many trails are maintained by the **Forestry Department**. Contact the Forestry Department *(173 Constant Spring Road, Kingston; tel: (809) 924-2667)* to book cabins, such as those at Hollywell National Recreation Area (see page 34), which has fine trails.

Maya Lodge and Hiking Centre, at Jack's Hill, is a traditional starting-point for Blue Mountain hikes. Several trails branch out from here. Maya is the home base of the **Jamaica Alternative Camping and Hiking Association** *(PO Box 216, Kingston; tel: (809) 927–2097)*, which can provide information on trails and accommodations, plus *A Hiker's Guide to the Blue Mountains*, by Bill Wilcox. Maya has campsites, cabins, and a café; campers have use of the kitchen. **Pine Grove** *(c/o 62 Duke Street, Kingston; tel: (809) 922–8705)*, a 23-acre plantation with guesthouse, and **Whitfield Hall**, an 8-mile uphill walk from Mavis Bank, also arrange guides and provide accommodations for hikers. (See also **Blue Mountain Hike**, page 42).

Plans are afoot to complete the Grand Ridge of the Blue Mountains trail that would link trails from the official starting point at Morces Gap, in the west, with the John Crow Mountains. Vinegar Hill Trail crosses the Blue Mountains north to south from Chepstowe, near Buff Bay, ending in Kingston. The route takes in Cinchona, Catherine's Peak, and Hollywell. Another rugged trail leads from Bath Fountain across the John Crows to Millbank, 20 miles south of Port Antonio. You can even make the arduous hike to Nanny Town after paying a courtesy call on the Maroon Colonel in Moore Town – he can arrange a guide.

The Fairy Glades and Fern Walk trails above Newcastle invite hikers to discover flora and fauna unique to

montane cloud forest.

The Malvern Hills near Mandeville are another popular hiking spot. Trails also lace the Hellshire Hills. Much of the Cockpit Country remains unexplored and trail-less; it is not wise to hike alone. It should be possible to hire a guide in Windsor, from where a trail leads to Troy.

Another trail established by JATCHA begins at Sign Great House, east of Montego Bay, and follows the Montego River. Sign is headquarters of the **Touring Society of Jamaica** (*Sign, PO Box 5, St James; tel: (809) 952-9188*), which offers information on hiking and guide services.

The **Jamaica Survey Department** (*23 1/2 Charles Street, Kingston; tel: (809) 922-6630*) publishes 1:50,000 topographical maps.

HILTON HIGH DAY TOUR

This is perhaps the most uplifting tour on the island. Known as the "Up, Up, and Buffet" tour, it includes a brief ride in a tethered hot-air balloon. Your venue is a 360-acre former banana plantation, Hilton, in St Leonards, reached via a scenic drive from Montego Bay. The hilltop location overlooks the German settlement at Seaford, visited as part of your day in the country. A buffet lunch is highlighted by roast suckling pig. *For information contact Hilton High, PO Box 162, Reading, Montego Bay; tel: (809) 952-3343). Tuesday, Friday, and Sunday, 9am–5pm.*

RIVER RAFTING

A leisurely raft trip is guaranteed to add romance to any Jamaica vacation. Swashbuckling movie hero Errol Flynn is credited with initiating rafting, on the Rio Grande, as a fun-filled tourist attraction. It was later encouraged by the Earl of Mansfield, who built a restaurant and pavilion at Rafter's Rest, the terminal of the journey once made by banana boatpeople. Today rafting is a well-established, well-organized attraction.

Rafting trips are offered on the Rio Grande in Port Antonio, the White River near Ocho Rios, and the Great River and Martha Brae River near Montego Bay. Each journey is like drifting through Shangri La. Each river threads down through green mountains, with trees arching overhead and vaulting cliffs that occasionally fall dark to the water.

Your transportation is a long, narrow bamboo raft with a raised double-seat, about two-thirds back. You are propelled by the gentle flow and a stout bamboo pole deftly wielded by the licensed raftsperson, who stands near the front with water washing his or her feet. Sometimes the water is shallow, clear and green, and mountain pure. At other times it is high, and you may swim next to the raft in deep, cool pools.

A bar-raft may sidle up beside you to offer rum punch, refreshing Red Stripe beer, or tourist trinkets (even on the river the hagglers are present).

Cattle graze the margins, while egrets and herons stand silently fishing for freshwater shrimp. You may even round a bend to find a band that will break into a calypso tune for your benefit.

The best rafting is the 6-mile, 2 1/2-hour journey down the Rio Grande. The trip begins at either Grants Level or Berridale, from where you drift to the river mouth at Rafter's Rest. Your car will have been driven to Rafter's Rest to

A lovely way to see the scenery

await you. For information contact Rio Grande Attractions, PO Box 128, Port Antonio (tel: (809) 993–2778).

Shorter trips on the Martha Brae (Martha Brae Rafting, tel: (809) 952–0889) and Great River (Mountain Valley Rafting, tel: (809) 952-0527) offer a 1-hour glide. They begin at Rafters Village, south of Falmouth and Lethe, respectively. The Great River trip includes a midday stop at a scenic recreation area, where you can enjoy donkey rides and laze in a hammock, drinking coconut milk or your favorite cocktail. The White River trip takes 45 minutes, including a short swimming stop at Calypso Cove (Calypso Rafting, tel: (809) 974-2527).

Superb yachting cruises are one of the major draws of the Caribbean, and Jamaica is no exception

NATIONAL PARKS

Jamaica has recently created the Protected Areas Resource Conservation Authority (PARC) and the Natural Resources Conservation Authority (NRCA) to protect the island's natural resources.

Creation of **Montego Bay Marine Park** in 1990 reflects the commitment. The sanctuary safeguards the shore and coastal waters from the Donald Sangster International Airport to the Great River. Water sports are available in designated areas. **Blue Mountains and John Crow National Park** protects 195,527 acres of endangered forest habitat. There are many scenic walking trails.

Ghourie State Park has many woodland trails that give rare access to the southeastern corner of the Cockpit Country. Spelunking is possible inside Ghourie Caves. A 1-day Ghourie Cave and Forest Reserve expedition is offered by **Calypso Island Tours**, *3901 Grand Avenue Suite 304, Oakland, CA 94610,* *USA (tel: 1–800–852–6242).*

SAILING TRIPS

Choose from a plethora of yachting cruises available in major resort areas. In Montego Bay options include the ***Mary Ann*** *(tel: (809) 952–5510)*, a 57-foot ketch that departs from Sandals, Montego Bay Resort; ***Montrose II***, which casts off from Pier 1 on Howard Cooke Highway courtesy of Rapsody Cruises *(tel: (809) 979-0104)*; and ***Calico*** *(tel: (809) 952–5860)*, a 55-foot wooden ketch that sets sail on day trips Tuesday to Sunday and sunset cruises Wednesday to Saturday. Ocho Rios's options include ***Cool Jazz***, Jamaica's largest and fastest catamaran, operated by Heave-Ho Fun Cruises *(tel: (809) 974–5367)*. The ***Margarita*** sails from Ocho Rios to No Problem Cove; *contact MC Tours (tel: (809) 974–1129).* A "Jolly Roger Cruise" aboard the ***Tironga*** lets you party with pirates *(tel: (809) 874–2323).*

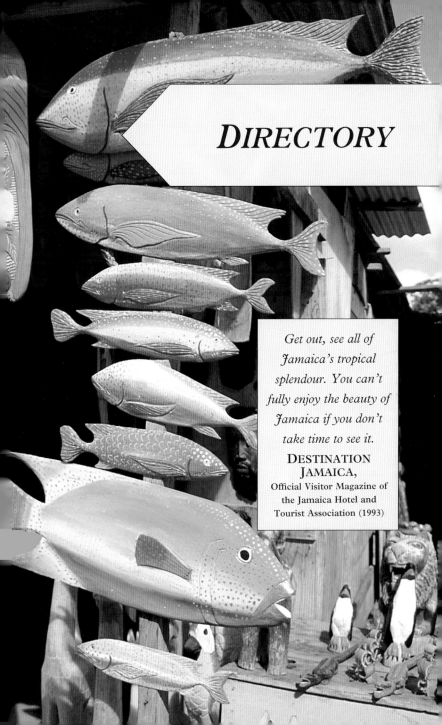

DIRECTORY

Get out, see all of Jamaica's tropical splendour. You can't fully enjoy the beauty of Jamaica if you don't take time to see it.

DESTINATION JAMAICA,
Official Visitor Magazine of the Jamaica Hotel and Tourist Association (1993)

Shopping

*J*amaica offers much for those who like to strike a bargain, be it a duty-free camera, hand-rolled cigars, an almost nonexistent bikini, a wood carving, or a fine piece of art hard-won from a "higgler."

Islandwide there are craft stalls and marketplaces where you can try your hand at the Jamaican sport of "higgling" (see **Markets**, page 144). Bargaining is a way of life here – negotiate! Never pay the asking price except in formal establishments.

The island also boasts many shopping centers where you can find everything from pottery to electronics. Do not be lured to particular stores by hired drivers or guides who often receive commissions.

Jamaica has no sales tax.

Clothing
Jamaica has a handful of fashionable designers producing chic day and evening wear using batik and silk-screen fabrics. Ivy Ralph's Designs, in Devon House, Kingston, has beautiful shirts and skirts made from African fabrics. Ubiquitous T-shirts tout the virtues of reggae, Rastafarianism, and *ganja* (marijuana). Kids will love a T-shirt of Mickey Mouse with his hair in dreadlocks!

Duty-free Shops
Jamaica is full of duty-free shops selling "in-bond" china, crystal, watches, perfume, and designer leather goods. Savings run from ten to forty percent. Check prices at home beforehand. In-bond items must be purchased in foreign currency and picked up at airports or piers as you leave. You can buy at duty-free stores in the airport departure lounges. An airline ticket and identification are required.

Souvenirs
You have never seen so many crafts in your life! The government-sponsored Things Jamaican shops offer the finest crafts: antique furniture reproductions, embroidered napkins, wooden salad bowls, pewter kitchenware, and so on. Craft markets tend towards straw goods, wood carvings, shell craft, hammocks, and T-shirts. Quality varies. Many are first-rate and make evocative mementoes.

Jamaica's fine art is remarkable. Several galleries display art pieces that sell for thousands of dollars.

There is plenty of jewelry, both trinket and designer variety. Beware so-called "gold" jewelry. It may be fake. Avoid black coral, shell, crocodile, and tortoiseshell items – they are illegal!

Don't leave without some delectable Blue Mountain Coffee, world-famous Appleton or Myers's rum, and perhaps Rumona rum liqueur, Tia Maria coffee liqueur, Sangster's pimento, Jamaican ginger, or ortanique liqueur.

KINGSTON
Devon House
The home of Things Jamaican. Shops sell everything from furniture, ceramics, and tableware to Jamaican liquors, baskets, T-shirts, and lace. *26 Hope Road (tel: (809) 929–7029). Open: Monday–Saturday, 9am–5:45pm.*

New Kingston Shopping Centre
A chic mall with thirty-seven stores, including fashion boutiques, within

walking distance of major hotels. *30
Dominica Drive, New Kingston. Open:
Monday–Saturday, 10am–6pm.*

Frame Centre Gallery
One of Jamaica's best collections of fine
art. *10 Tangerine Place, Kingston (tel:
(809) 926–4644).*

THE WEST
Mo'Bay's main duty-free shopping
complexes are at **Montego Freeport**,
City Centre, and **Holiday Village**,
directly across from the Holiday Inn.
Half Moon Village, 4 miles east of
Montego Bay, is a new shopping plaza
covering 7 acres. Negril has minishops at
the **Plaza de Negril** in the town center;
crafts abound on the beach and along
West End Road.

Gallery of West Indian Art
This showcase of fine Jamaican art brims
with paintings, carvings, and pottery.
Some fifty artists contribute. *1 Orange
Lane, Montego Bay (tel: (809) 952–4547).*

Things Jamaican
The very best of Jamaican arts, crafts,
and foodstuffs. *44 Fort Street, Montego
Bay (tel: (809) 952–1936).*

NORTH COAST
Shopping centers in Ocho Rios include
Mutual Security Plaza, **Island Plaza**,
Coconut Grove, **Pineapple Place**, and
Ocean Village, home to the straw
market, next to Turtle Beach Towers.

Harmony Hall
Its Gallery of Jamaican Art showcases the
finest of arts and crafts, as well as
liqueurs, food items, and figurines. *On
the A3, 4 miles east of Ocho Rios (tel:
(809) 975–4222).*

Wood carvings at Pineapple Place, Ocho Rios

Gallery Joe James
Naïve paintings, carvings, and masks
from one of Jamaica's most famous
artists. *Hotel Rio Bueno, Rio Bueno.*

Caribatik Island Fabrics
Rainbow-hued, hand-batiked silk
clothes, cotton wall-hangings, and art.
*Rock Wharf, 2 miles east of Falmouth (tel:
(809) 954–3314).*

Ruth Claridge
Distinctive hand-screened cotton
creations, many hand-embroidered.
*Ocean Village Shopping Centre, Ocho Rios
(tel: (809) 974–2874).*

THE EAST
Designer's Gallery
Top-notch locally produced art, crafts,
clothing, and jewelry. Run by Patrice
Wymore Flynn, widow of Hollywood
legend Errol Flynn. *Jamaica Palace Hotel,
Port Antonio (tel: (809) 993–3294).*

Freeport Giftland
A complex of duty-free shops. *City Centre
Plaza, Port Antonio (tel: (809)
993–2716).*

MARKETS

designed to foil pickpockets. They keep most of their money safe in cloth "threadbags" buried deep in their bosoms, along with garlic or grains of corn as charms against thieves. You, too, should stay alert about your personal items.

Uniquely Jamaican markets, such as Papine, at the east end of Hope Road, are scattered throughout Kingston. Go with a local guide. Coronation Market, the island's largest, overflows North and South Parade. Wooden handcarts and rickety wooden stalls are

"**C**an I sell you somelin' sweet, darlin'," calls a jubilant woman in colorful garb. Carrots, shallots, beets, grapefruit, mangoes, and sugarcane stripped down to its juicy core are spread out in brilliant display. You are surrounded by a whirligig of petty trading. Welcome to a public market – a fairground of color and sound – where "hagglers" (street pedlars) hawk their wares.

Every town has a public market, best visited late in the week when the activity is more intense. The scene generally looks like a little piece of Africa. The open-air markets abound in yams and turnips, lima-bean-like gungo peas, squash and pumpkins, breadfruit and ackee, garlic and onions, and tiny red, fiery peppers.

"Market Mammies" are queens of the trade. Their uniform is a "bib," a large apron, with two deep pockets

stacked high with produce, mountains of brassières, and even scrap salvaged from the corporation dump, or "dungle."

The Montego Bay Public Market is on Fustic Street. In Port Antonio check out Musgrave Market, a great place to purchase Blue Mountain coffee, eye-catching leatherwork, tropical flower perfumes, and a wide range of touristy souvenirs.

There is no lack of choice in the street markets of Jamaica

Every resort has a lively craft market for tourists. Offerings run from hand-woven baskets, straw hats, and Jamaica-shaped key chains to etched gourds, T-shirts, and hammocks.

Mo'Bay's Crafts Market, on Howard Cook Boulevard at Fort Street, is one of the largest. Nearby is the Old Fort Craft Park, behind the fort on Gloucester Avenue. Vendors are licensed by the Jamaica Tourist Board.

The straw market at Ocean Village in Ocho Rios offers a special bounty of straw hats, place mats, rugs, and the like. The items are made here from palm fronds or the straw of jipijapa, the plant of which Panama hats are made. The best bargains are found after cruise passengers have returned to their ships. Wood-carving stalls atop Dunn's River Falls display creations in mahogany, ebony, and lignum vitae (a rose-colored hardwood).

The Negril Crafts Park, at the junction of Norman Manley Boulevard and West End Road, is terrific for wooden carvings and T-shirts. Kingston's Victoria Crafts Market, Port Royal Street near Victoria Pier, is less expensive than more touristy markets.

Most craft markets are open Monday–Friday, 8am–5pm; Saturday, 8am–6pm.

Entitlement

*T*ame by day, Jamaica gets down by night. From reggae to opera, the options are many. There are nightclubs, of course, but also calm, torchlit river rafting trips under the moonlight, topped off by dinner and entertainment on the riverbank. Most larger hotels have nightly floorshows to keep guests amused. This tends towards limbo and Carnival-style "junkanoo" dancers, live calypso bands, and Caribbean theme parties.

When you have had your fill of theme nights, throw on your T-shirt and get ready to jam at any of hundreds of discos nationwide. Many larger hotels have their own nightclubs where non-guests are welcome. Even the most remote village has its "disco," which may be a set of speakers (usually of unbelievable size) tied to a tree.

In Mo'Bay outside parties keep the party going – the streets vibrate with DeeJay music, *ganja* (marijuana) smoke hangs thick in the air, and you will dance shoulder-to-sweaty-shoulder with a mostly Jamaican crowd. Where you land depends on what night it is. Leave jewelry and purses in your hotel safety-deposit box.

Kingston is Jamaica's cultural center, with a lively tradition of performing arts, including classical symphony, choral, folk music, and classical and contemporary dance. Kingston, too, is famous for its lively pantomime season when satirical vignettes spoof current affairs.

Jamaica hosts many festivals of world renown. Every summer, it hosts two of the largest music gatherings in the world: Reggae Sunsplash, in Kingston, and Reggae Sumfest, in Montego Bay. Traditional "Jonkanoo" celebrations, held each Christmas, feature float parades and street dancing hotter than the tropical night.

Sunset is absolutely free. In Negril it is almost a religious experience, and tourists flock nightly like lemmings to Rick's Cafe to watch the sun slide from view.

The Jamaica Tourist Board publishes a *Calendar of Events* and can provide information on up-to-date happenings. *The Daily Gleaner* publishes a listing of events and venues. In Kingston check with *High Times, Shop 42, Kingston Mall (tel: (809) 922–5538),* for information on the local scene.

BOONOONOONOOS

The patois word means "great." More specifically it means "beach party," at which Jamaicans excel. These vary from well-organized family affairs to bacchanals with virtual X-rated dancing! Live reggae music, plus open bar and buffet dinner are staples. On weekends you can "ride de riddims" with the locals at **Fort Clarence Beach**, west of Kingston. Other Boonoonoonoos include:

Boonoonoonoos Beach Party, *Walter Fletcher Beach, Montego Bay (tel: (809) 952-5719), every Friday, 7pm.*
Cornwall Beach Party, *Cornwall Beach, Montego Bay, every Monday, 7pm.*
Dead End Jam, *Kent Avenue, Montego Bay, every Thursday.*
Jamaican Night on the White River, *(tel: (809) 974–2619), every Thursday and Sunday, 7pm.*

An audience at a Soca Band Concert getting in the swing of things

Lollypop on the Beach, *at Sandy Bar near Tryall (tel: (809) 952–4121), every Wednesday and Saturday, 7:30pm–11pm.*
Monday Night Carnival, *Gloucester Avenue, Montego Bay (tel: (809) 952–4425), every Monday, 7pm–12am.*
Reggae Lobster Party, *Coconut Grove Great House, 1 mile east of Ocho Rios (tel: (809) 974–5932), every Monday and Thursday, 7pm.*

CINEMAS
Strand Theatre, *8 Strand Street, Montego Bay (tel: (809) 952–5391).*
Carib Cinema, *Cross Roads, Kingston (tel: (809) 926–6106).*
Odeon Cinema, *Mandeville (tel: (809) 962–2177).*
Cineplex I & II, Sovereign Centre, *106 Hope Road, Kingston (tel: (809) 978–3522).*
Portmore Palace, *Portmore Mall, Portmore (tel: (809) 988–2720).*

CLASSICAL
The **Jamaica Philharmonic Symphony Orchestra** and **National Chorale Orchestra** perform at Kingston's Little Theatre, *4 Tom Redcam Avenue (tel: (809) 926–6129)*, and other venues.

The **Creative Arts Centre** *(tel: (809) 927-1047)* at the University of the West Indies at Mona hosts classical, popular, and folklore performances by the University Singers.

DANCE
The **National Dance Theatre Company** *(tel: (809) 926–6603)* performs its "Season of Dance" at the Little Theatre, July–August and December. A modern-dance company, **L'Acadco** (L'Antoinette Caribbean American Dance Company), offers a "Cabaret Repertoire," plus classical, modern, and folk forms. Venues vary.

MISCELLANEOUS

Bill's Place, Main Street, Ocho Rios, is a popular tourist hangout – the jukebox plays favorites from way-back-when. **The Ruins**, DaCosta Drive, Ocho Rios *(tel: (809) 974–2442)*, has varied entertainment – limbo, calypso, Caribbean dancing, and the like. A **Moonlick Party** is held at Firefly *(tel: (809) 997–7201)*, near Port Maria, each weekend closest to the full moon; jazz bands play at the open-air theater.

NIGHTCLUBS/DISCOTHEQUES

Jamaica's in-vogue dance style is called "wine on ah bumsee," which roughly translates as "to make sexual motions on a woman's behind." Considering the writhing groin-to-groin rhythm, you will be amazed that Jamaica's birth rate is no higher! *Note:* many local nightclubs feature bare-skin dancers performing *risqué* acts. Classier discos in Kingston traditionally offer "oldies" music on Sundays.

Kingston

24 K Night Club, *Manor Centre, 195 Constant Spring Road, Kingston 10 (tel: (809) 969–3253)*.
Bleachers Sports Bar and Grill, *7th Avenue Plaza, Kingston 10 (tel: (809) 926–3900)*.
Cactus, *13 Portmore Plaza, Portmore, west of Kingston (tel: (809) 988–2319)*.
Epiphany, *1 St Lucia Avenue, Kingston 5 (tel: (809) 929–1130)*.
Godfathers, *69 Knutsford Road (tel: (809) 929–5459)*.
Illusions, *Lane Plaza, 2–4 South Avenue, Kingston 10 (tel: (809) 926–7419)*.
Mingles, *The Courtleigh, 31 Trafalgar Road, Kingston 10 (tel: (809) 926–8174)*.

Montego Bay

Disco Inferno, *Holiday Village, east of Montego Bay (tel: (809) 953–2113)*.
Jonkanoo Lounge, *Wyndham Rose Hall Beach Hotel (tel: (809) 953–2650)*.
Lyle's Intensified Inn, *36 Barnett Street (tel: (809) 952–4980)*.
Pier 1, *Howard Cooke Boulevard (tel: (809) 952–2452)*.
The Cave, *Seawind Beach Resort, Montego Freeport (tel: (809) 952–4874)*.
Sir Winstons Reggae Club, *Kent Avenue (tel: (809) 952–2084)*.
Witch's Hideaway, *Holiday Inn, east of Montego Bay (tel: (809) 953–2485)*.

Mandeville

Tracks, *Mandeville Shopping Plaza*.

Negril

Close Encounter, *3 King's Plaza (tel: (809) 957–4032)*.
Compulseion, *Plaza de Negril (tel: (809) 957–4416)*.
De Buss, *Norman Manley Boulevard (tel: (809) 957–4405)*.
Private Affair Disco, *Hotel Samsara, West End Road (tel: (809) 957–4395)*.
Hedonism II, *Norman Manley Boulevard (tel: (809) 957–4200)*.

Ocho Rios

Acropolis, *Mutual Security Building, 70 Main Street (tel: (809) 974–2633)*.
Jamaica'N Me Crazy, *Jamaica Grande Hotel, Main Street (tel: (809) 974–2201)*.
Little Pub, *Main Street (tel: (809) 974–2324)*.
Roof Nightclub, *7 James Avenue (tel: (809) 974–1042)*.
Silks Nightclub, *Shaw Park Beach Hotel, 4 miles east of Ocho Rios (tel: (809) 974–2552)*.

Port Antonio

Roof Club, *11 West Street (tel: (809)*

993-3817).
Taurus Club, *Somerset Street.*

Runaway Bay
Banana's Fun Bar and Grill, *(tel: (809) 973–2006).*
Stinger Disco, *Tamarind Tree Hotel (tel: (809) 973–2678).*

PIANO BARS and PUBS

Pubs and piano bars offer a break from the disco beat. Many major resorts have pub-style lounges.

Bill Laurie's Steak House, *Bloomfield Gardens, Mandeville (tel: (809) 962–3116).*
Doctor's Cave Beach Hotel, *Gloucester Avenue, Montego Bay (tel: (809) 952–4355).*
Hemingway's Pub, *36 Gloucester Avenue, Montego Bay (tel: (809) 952-8606).*
Mandeville Arms, *Mandeville Hotel, Mandeville (tel: (809) 962-2460).*
The Pegasus Hotel, *81 Knutsford Boulevard, Kingston (tel: (809) 926-3690).*

REGGAE CONCERTS

Jamaica has hundreds of local reggae bands. You are sure to find one or more playing on weekends at beach parties on the Hellshire Beaches near Kingston. Negril has taken over from Kingston as the island's live reggae capital – there always seems to be some big talent in town. The sounds of Ziggy Marley, Burning Spear, and other top rankin' reggae stars mingle with the sound of the surf. Popular venues in Negril include:
Hotel Sam Sara, *West End Road (tel: (809) 957-4395).*
Kaiser's, *West End Road (tel: (809) 957–4070), Wednesday and Friday.*
Mandela Green, *Green Island, 2 miles*

north of Negril *(tel: (809) 956–9126).*
MXIII Entertainment Centre, *West End Road (tel: (809) 957–4827), Thursday and Saturday.*
Tree House Club, *Norman Manley Boulevard (tel: (809) 957–4287).*

SHOWS

Bistro Macaw, *Montego Bay (tel: (809) 979–3911),* dinner theater/club cabaret.
Little Pub, *Main Street, Ocho Rios (tel: (809) 974–2324),* nightly shows billed as Broadway-style revues. Touristy, but fun. Entertainment includes *The Mighty Digger*, an Afro-Caribbean musical adapted from the play *Ipi-N-Tambia*, and *Ocho Rios! Ocho Rios!*, a fully Jamaican musical, including female performers in swimsuits.
Negril Tree House Club, *Norman Manley Boulevard, Negril (tel: (809) 957–4287),* floor show, Monday.
Fern Hill, *Port Antonio (tel: (809) 993–3222),* folklore show, Friday.

THEATER

Kingston has a flourishing drama scene, with a choice of productions at major theaters most nights of the year. Local theaters fill in the gaps.
Barn Theatre, *5 Oxford Road, Kingston (tel: (809) 926–6469).*
Little Theatre, *4 Tom Redcam Avenue, Kingston (tel: (809) 926–6129).* The National Dance Theatre Company, Jamaica's most highly acclaimed theater company, perform July–August. The Jamaica Folk Singers stage a major presentation in March and April.
New Kingston Theatre, *Altamont Crescent (tel: (809) 929–2618).*
Ward Theatre, *North Parade, Kingston (tel: (809) 922–0543).* The National Pantomime Musical is performed during the winter season (December to spring).

Festivals and Events

January

Jamaica Philharmonic Choral Group Concert Season, Courtleigh Hotel, Kingston *(tel: (809) 926–0801)*.

Accompong Maroon Festival, Accompong, St. Elizabeth *(tel: (809) 952–4546)*. Annual celebration with dancing, singing, feasting, and traditional ceremonies.

Negril Sprint Triathlon, Negril. Features swimming, cycling, and a foot race, organized by the Jamaica Triathlon Federation. For information contact JTB offices.

High Mountain 10K Road Race, Williamsfield *(tel: (809) 963–4211)*. Largest road race in Jamaica.

February

Pineapple Cup Yacht Race, Montego Bay Yacht Club. An annual 811-mile race from Miami to Montego Bay.

Bob Marley Birthday Bash, Bob Marley Museum, Kingston *(tel: (809) 923–9380)*. Annual celebration featuring the world's top reggae artists.

Sugar Cane Ball, Round Hill Hotel, Montego Bay *(tel: (809) 952–5150)*. An annual cocktail party followed by a grand ball in aid of charity. Dust off your DJ!

Chukka Cove Appleton Cup, Chukka Cove, near Ocho Rios *(tel: (809) 972-2506)*. Top international players compete in this 14-goal polo tournament.

University of West Indies Carnival, Kingston *(tel: (809) 927-4870)*. Carnival with steel bands, reggae bands, soca jump-up, and crowning of the Carnival King and Queen.

March

Negril West End Reggae Festival, Hog Heaven Hotel Complex, Negril *(tel: (809) 957–4991)*. Reggae superstars perform atop the cliffs!

April

Jamaica Polo Association Tournament and Horse Show, Chukka Cove, near Ocho Rios *(tel: (809) 972–2506)*. Combined event with top polo players from around the world.

Easter Craft Fair, Harmony Hall, Ocho Rios *(tel: (809) 975–4222)*. Jamaica's leading artists display their works; live entertainment.

Jamaica Carnival, Ocho Rios and Kingston. Top calypso and reggae performers, plus street parades with costumed groups, soca parties, and so on.

University Singers Concert Season, University of the West Indies, Kingston *(tel: (809) 927–1877)*. Presentation of Jamaican folk songs, choral music, and classical and popular selections.

May

South Coast Fishing Tournament, Black River *(tel: (809) 965–2074)*. A 3-day event for fishing enthusiasts.

Manchester Horticultural Society Show, Mandeville *(tel: (809) 962–2909)*. Displays of flowers and plants.

June

Ocho Rios Jazz Festival, Ocho Rios *(tel: (809) 927–3544)*. Annual, week-long series of concerts by local and international jazz greats.

All-Jamaica Tennis Championships, Kingston *(tel: 1–800–233–4JTB)*. Combination of tennis competitions, from the Couples Junior Classic to the

Red Stripe All-Jamaica Championship.

White River Reggae Bash, White River, St Ann *(tel: (809) 974-2619)*. Jamaica's leading reggae stars perform along the banks of the White River.

July

Manchester Golf Week, Manchester Club, Mandeville *(tel: (809) 975-4287)*. Jamaica's oldest golf tournament, attracting leading local and international players.

August

Independence Celebrations *(tel: (809) 926-5726)*. Islandwide events, including a gala street parade in Kingston. Traditional Jonkanoo dancers, as well as modern dancers, showcase a cross-section of Jamaican culture.

Reggae Sunsplash, Jamworld, Caymanas, Kingston *(tel: (809) 942-2009 or 1-800-WE-SPLASH)*. World-famous outdoor reggae festival, featuring 5 nights of music.

Reggae Sumfest, Bob Marley Performing Centre, Montego Bay *(tel: (809) 979-1720)*. Mo'Bay's answer to Reggae Sunsplash, featuring world-class reggae stars.

Portland Jamboree, Port Antonio. Nine days of street dancing, art shows, a float parade, and reggae singers. For information contact JTB offices.

September

Miss Jamaica World Beauty Pageant, National Arena, Kingston *(tel: (809) 927-7575)*. Pageant deciding who will represent Jamaica in the Miss World Contest.

Montego Bay International Marlin Tournament, Montego Bay Yacht Club *(tel: (809) 979-8038)*. An annual game-fishing tournament, begun in 1967.

October

Port Antonio International Marlin Fishing Tournament, Port Antonio Marina *(tel: (809) 923-8724)*. One of the oldest and most prestigious game-fishing tournaments in the Caribbean.

Jamaica Open Pepsi Pro-Am Golf Tournament, Wyndham Rose Hall, Montego Bay *(tel: (809) 925-2325)*. Pro-am event attracting top club pros from North America and the UK.

All smiles at the Kingston Festival

November

Jamaica Golf Week. A series of pro-am golf events around the island. For information contact JTB offices worldwide.

December

Johnnie Walker World Golf Championship, Tryall Golf Club, Montego Bay *(tel: (809) 956-5600)*. Annual event at which the top twenty-eight golf pros in the world vie for the largest purse in professional golf.

Mongoose Open Champagne Brunch, Chukka Cove, Ocho Rios *(tel: (809) 972-2506)*. A fun polo tournament where the players dress in costume.

SUNSPLASH

For 6 days each summer Jamaica commands the world music stage. Legions of reggae fans flock from every corner of the globe. Hotels sell out. And 100,000 joyous revellers dance beneath the stars to the syncopated rhythms of the world's most irresistible beat.

Since its inception in 1978 Reggae Sunsplash has established itself as the world's premier reggae event. Since 1981, when Stevie Wonder sang ". . . didn't know you would be jammin' until the break of dawn," Sunsplash has become an all-night affair. The nonstop narcotic beat keeps the masses dancing and swaying until the sun rises above the calm Caribbean. Clouds of *ganja* (marijuana) swirl above the crowd. And the sensation of "one love" – the creed of racial harmony coined by the late reggae legend Bob Marley –

is palpable as the trouble-free crowd undulates hip-to-hip to the sensual dusk-to-dawn orgy of music.

For over a decade Sunsplash was held in Montego Bay. In 1993 it returned to its roots in Kingston, the birthplace of reggae and its origins, Rocksteady and Ska. The purpose-built venue, Jamworld Festival Village, has redeemed Kingston's reputation as the cultural hub and the most exciting city in the Caribbean. The setting on the banks of the Rio Cobre (with the Blue Mountains and Kingston's city lights twinkling across the harbor as a backdrop) is marvellous.

Montego Bay now has a new event, Reggae Sumfest, which began in summer 1993 at the Bob Marley Entertainment Centre.

Sunsplash begins with an all-night beach party at Fort Clarence Beach, Hellshire. Each night has a distinct musical theme: Vintage Night and International Night, for example, and Dance Hall, the in-vogue reggae beat that melds rap with reggae. Steel Pulse, England's reggae maestros, are frequent performers. So, too, are Burning Spear, Third World, Toots and The Maytals, Ziggy Marley, Shabba Ranks, and other reggae greats.

"Ridin de riddims" at Reggae Sunsplash and Reggae Sumfest

If you go wear loose, lightweight clothing and comfortable shoes. Otherwise you cannot "ride de riddims." Take a sweater or jacket in case the night turns cool. A cushion, stool, or mat is useful. Sleep through the preceding afternoon.

For further information contact **Synergy Productions**, 23 Stony Hill Road, Kingston 8 *(tel: (809) 942–2009, or 1–800–WE–SPLASH)*. For organized Sunsplash tours contact **Music Travel Centre** in London *(tel: 071–383 7518)*. In the USA contact **Calypso Island Tours**, 3901 Grand Avenue, Suite 304, Oakland, CA 94610 *(tel: 1–800–852–6242 or 510–653–3570)*. Make your reservations well in advance.

Children

*J*amaicans adore children. Amusement parks and other commercial kiddie's attractions are almost nonexistent. Local young people have fun at the beach, in rivers and streams, and by playing with makeshift bat and ball.

ANANCY FUN PARK

Jamaica's only theme park features go-carts, an 18-hole miniature golf course, a carousel, a fishing pond, boating, nature trails, and donkey cart and jeep rides. It is opposite the Poinciana Beach Hotel in Negril (see below).

BEACHES

Bring a bucket and spade – your children will want to spend countless hours on the beach. The calm, shallow waters are perfect for young ones. Pedal-boats and other water sports, including children's snorkeling, are widely available. Avoid areas of coral, as well as the wave-battered east coast. And guard against too much sun!

Schoolboy at Hagley Gap

HOTELS

Many hotels welcome children and have play directors and supervised activities. Some cater to family vacations with comprehensive program and facilities for children. Children under 12 (sometimes under 14 or 16) generally stay free when overnighting with parents. Many hotels can arrange cots (cribs) at no extra charge. Most can arrange baby-sitters by advance request; advise the hotel of your requirements when you make your reservation. Consider a villa, which gives you absolute freedom and may prove most cost-effective for large families. Some villa operators arrange for nannies to stay overnight.

Boscobel Beach

Boscobel, *PO Box 63, Ocho Rios (tel: (809) 974–3330)*, bills itself as "a family paradise." The all-inclusive family resort is lots of fun for young people. Facilities include donkey rides, a petting zoo, a camping area, clowns and cotton candy, craft classes, reggae dance lessons, video games and a computer lab, plus special kids' meals. Children under 14 stay free in their parents' room. A special wing is reserved for adults only. SuperNannies look after the kids.

Franklin D Resort

This all-suites, all-inclusive resort, *PO Box 201, Runaway Bay, St Ann (tel: (809) 973–3067)*, is geared to families

Meet the local kids – it looks like fun!

with children under 16. Children stay, eat, and play at no charge. Each Mediterranean-style villa comes with a specially trained Girl Friday who combines maid duties with child-care and baby-sitting. A Kiddie's Centre features a computer center, a toddler's disco, plus arts and crafts. Special children's programs help keep kids amused while you indulge in a panoply of adult activities. The beach is very narrow, but water sports are on hand to indulge your children and the child in you.

Poinciana Beach Hotel
Poinciana, *Norman Manley Boulevard, Negril (tel: (809) 957–4100)*, is Negril's only "family resort." You can drop the kids off to enjoy the Kiddies Playhouse under the watchful eye of a Kids' Coordinator while you learn to windsurf. Poinciana has over 1,000 feet of beach, plus the Anancy Theme Park (see above).

JAMAICA SAFARI VILLAGE
Crocodile feeding time is sure to keep rapt. The park has a petting zoo and bird sanctuary, plus snakes and mongooses, as well as a breeding center and crocodile ponds. Conducted tours are offered. *Tel: (809) 954–3065. Admission charge. Open: daily, 8:30am–5:30pm. 2 miles west of Falmouth.*

MEETING LOCAL KIDS
If you would like your child or children to meet local kids, consider staying with a Jamaican family. The Jamaican Tourist Board's Meet the People program (see **First Steps**) will match you with a family of similar ages and interests. Alternatively contact *Community Tourism, c/o Astra Country Inn, 62 Ward Avenue, Mandeville (tel: (809) 962-3265)*, which can also match you for overnight stays.

MISCELLANEOUS
Supermarkets all over the island stock baby milk, children's food, and plenty of diapers.

The JTB publication *Things To Know Before You Go* lists attractions that offer children's discounts.

Sports

*J*amaica's realm of sports is inexhaustible, whether on or under land or in, on, or under water. While you may be astonished to learn that Jamaica has an Olympic bob-sled team, this is one of the few activities you will not find offered.

The possibilities will keep you busy, whether you choose an invigorating horseback ride, a tennis grand slam, or a round of golf in the footsteps of the pros. Virtually all the beaches have watersports, including sailing, game fishing, windsurfing, and waterskiing. And you can slip on your snorkel or scuba gear and discover a Jamaica that is as beautiful below as it is above.

Major resort hotels offer sports fitness centers. Negril's 10-acre Swept Away is the most comprehensive, with 10 floodlit tennis courts, a 25m swimming pool, an aerobics center, air-conditioned squash,

racquetball and basketball courts, and a jogging path centerd in and around the Sports and Fitness Complex. It is open to the public for a small fee.

Spectator sports are meagre.

BOATING

Most resorts offer Sunfish or Sailfish – small boats ideal for playing around in close to shore. Larger boats may be chartered from yacht clubs in Kingston, Montego Bay, and Port Royal. Make sure operators are licensed by the Jamaica Tourist Board. For information contact the **Royal Jamaica Yacht Club** *(tel: (809) 924–8685)* in Kingston; **Morgan's Harbour Marina** *(tel: (809) 924–8464)* in Port Royal; or the **Montego Bay Yacht Club** *(tel: (809) 979–8038)*. In Port Antonio boat rentals are available through **Huntress Marina**, *16 West St. (tel: (809) 993–3053)*.

GAME FISHING

Beyond the reefs Jamaica's waters are a pelagic playpen. Beginning as close as a mile and a half offshore the ocean floor plummets to immeasurable depths, marking the edge of the Cayman Trench, the deepest region in the entire Caribbean. Known as "Marlin Alley," it is a migratory path for prized blue marlin and other deepwater game fish – yellowfin tuna, wahoo, kingfish, and

Relaxing in style at the Montego Bay Sandals Resort

barracuda – that run through these waters year-round.

Jamaica boasts three primary fishing centers: Ocho Rios, Port Antonio, and Montego Bay. Half- and full-day charters can be booked through most major hotels. No licenses are required. Most boats accommodate up to six passengers. Most skippers expect a fifty percent deposit and 24 hours advance reservation. Book only through the skipper or crew member, *never* with bystanders on the dock. Charter boats usually keep fifty percent of the catch.

Jamaica hosts several blue marlin tournaments, topped by the annual International Marlin Tournament of Port Antonio. Held every October since 1963, it is one of the oldest and most prestigious game fishing tournaments in the Caribbean. The best time for marlin is September to April, with prize catches usually caught between June and August.

GOLF

Jamaica is blessed with rippling green fairways that border the blue Caribbean. Golf is Jamaica's great sporting strength. Jamaica has more courses than any other Caribbean island. Booking ahead is essential. Carts are available at most courses, as are caddies, who carry golf bags on their heads!

Jamaica's first course was established in the mid-1800s at Mandeville. It is a quaint 9-hole course with 18 tee positions located at the **Manchester Club** *(tel: (809) 962–2403)*, 2,200 feet up in the cool mountains.

The **Tryall Golf, Tennis and Beach Club** *(tel: (809) 956–5660)* is irrefutably the island's best course. The 6,920-yard, par 71 course is contoured on the site of an 18th-century sugar plantation. Tryall (an official PGA Tour approved course) hosts the world's richest purse – the $2.7 million Johnnie Walker World Championship.

Wyndham Rose Hall Country Club *(tel: (809) 953–2650)*, east of Montego Bay, is the venue for the PGA-sanctioned Jamaica Open. The prevailing winds and severe doglegs challenge even the most accomplished golfer. The 6,800-yard, par 72 course has magnificent sea views.

There are two other courses near Montego Bay: **Ironshore** *(tel: (809) 953–2800)*, a 6,570-yard, par 72, links-type course; and the Robert Trent Jones-designed championship course (7,119 yards, par 72) at **Half Moon** *(tel: (809) 953–2211)*.

Ocho Rios boasts two courses. **Sandals Golf and Country Club** *(tel: (809) 974–5691)* is owned by the Sandals resort chain. The 18-hole course (6,600 yards, par 71), formerly Upton Golf Club, is free to guests at any of Sandals' six properties. The resplendent **Runaway Bay** course *(tel: (809) 973–2561)* is another superb challenge (6,870 yards, par 72). It hosts the Superclubs Golf Invitational in September.

The **Jamaica Jamaica** resort *(tel: (809) 973–2436)* boasts the island's only golf school available to the public. The school, at Runaway Bay, caters to everyone from beginners to advanced golfers.

Kingston has two courses: **Caymanas** *(tel: (809) 997–8026)*, Jamaica's first 18-hole championship course, and **Constant Spring** *(tel: (809) 924–1610)*. At the time of writing, an 18-hole championship course was nearing completion 2 miles east of Negril. A new course was also under construction at Port Antonio.

Green fees range from $10 to $85. Clubs can be rented for about $20 a round.

Go horseback riding at Prospect Plantation

HORSEBACK RIDING

Stables throughout the island offer everything from polo matches to pony treks that guarantee a relaxing means of exploring offbeat Jamaica. Options range from canters along the coast to rugged rides into the mountains. Most hotels can arrange horseback riding through local stables.

Chukka Cove Farm is a complete equestrian center located between St Ann's and Runaway Bay. The facility offers beach rides, plus 1-, 2-, and 3-day treks led by experienced guides. Chukka Cove also features a full-sized polo field. Beginner lessons are available, as is instruction in dressage, show-jumping, and cross-country. *For information contact Chukka Cove, PO Box 160, Ocho Rios (tel: (809) 972–2506).*

The **Rocky Point Stables** *(tel: (809) 953–2286)* at the Half Moon Club, Montego Bay, also offers trail rides and riding lessons. At **Good Hope** *(tel: (809) 954-3289)*, near Falmouth, you can canter through orchards of coconut, papaya, and ugli; then dive into the Martha Brae and follow the streamside bridle path back to the old plantation.

Other estates that offer rides include **Prospect Plantation** *(tel: (809) 974–2373)*, near Ocho Rios; **Priestman's River Plantation**, the former estate of Errol Flynn near Port Antonio.

On the south coast is **Mayfield Ranch** *(tel: (809) 965–6234)*, where bridle paths unveil serene landscapes at 1,700-feet elevation above the shore near Lovers' Leap. In Kingston contact **Kingston Polo Club Riding Stables** *(tel: (809) 927–2473)*.

In Negril check with **Horseman Riding Stables** *(tel: (809) 957–4474)* or **Rhodes Hall Plantation**, which offers 2-hour rides through the estate and along the beach.

HORSE RACING

If you want to lay odds on a winner, horse racing takes place every Wednesday, Saturday, and public holidays at **Caymanas Park** *(tel: (809) 988–2523)*, near Kingston.

PARASAILING

You "fly" beneath a parachute attached to a speedboat churning along 100 feet below your dangling legs. If people had wings, it would be like this! Trips last 20 to 30 minutes and can be booked through water-sport concessions at every major beach resort.

SCUBA DIVING

Jamaica's shoreline waters quickly change from turquoise to royal blue to deep indigo. A single reef runs along the entire north coast. Water temperature averages 24 °C, with visibility from 70 to 120 feet.

Dozens of resorts and diving operators cater to the experienced diver. Novices can easily gain SCUBA

... or perhaps you prefer horse racing at Caymanas Park

certification while those already certified will find tanks widely available for rent. You must show a certification card to rent scuba gear or participate in guided diving trips.

Montego Bay is famous for its wall dives. Old Airport Reef is considered the best site on the island, known for its coral caves, tunnels, and canyons. Jacques Cousteau marvelled at its "dramatic sponge life." Local companies include **Montego Bay Divers**, **Poseidon Nimrod Divers** *(tel: (809) 952–3624)*, and **Reef Keeper Divers** *(tel: (809) 979–0104)*.

Between St Ann's Bay and Ocho Rios the wall is within swimming distance of shore. **PR Scuba Technologies** *(tel: (809) 974–1880)*, in St Ann's Bay, offers PADI certification and dive packages. Contact **Fantasea** *(tel: (809) 974–2353)* in Ocho Rios. **La Mer Dive and Beach Resort** *(tel: (809) 975–5002)*, 4 miles east of Ocho Rios, sits in front of the best diving site in Ocho Rios.

In Port Antonio **Navy Island Resort and Marina** *(tel: (809) 993-2667)* offers scuba lessons and rents diving equipment. Kingston Harbour is one of the Caribbean's best-kept secrets; Port Royal has sunken ships that provide a haven for a dense array of tropical fish. Contact **Morgan's Harbour Marine** *(tel: (809) 924–8464)*.

Negril offers Treasure Reef, where spotted moray eels will pose for your camera. **Negril Scuba Centre** *(tel: (809) 957–4425)*, in the Negril Beach Club Hotel, offers diving packages. Other options include **Dolphin Divers** *(tel: (809) 957–4944)* and **Blue Whale Divers** *(tel: (809) 957–4438)*.

If you've got all the gear you can scuba dive at St Ann's Bay

SPELUNKING (CAVING)

Jamaica is a spelunker's heaven. Almost two-thirds of the island is formed of limestone, much of it pock marked with caves. The Cockpit Country and north central Jamaica are replete with cave systems. Options range from well-known "show" caves, such as Windsor, Nonsuch, and Two Sisters Caves to hundreds of unexplored caves that will challenge the most intrepid spelunker.

Caves are poorly charted. Water levels can rise dramatically within minutes, and there is no cave rescue system. You enter at your own risk! Hire a guide and ensure you are well prepared with headlamps and other necessary equipment.

*For information contact the **Jamaica Caving Club**, c/o Dept of Geology, University of the West Indies, Mona, Kingston 7 (tel: (809) 927–6661).*

SURFING

Jamaica is not noted as a surfer's paradise, although substantial waves are found on the east coast. Boston Beach,

Just the weather for messing around in boats at Montego Bay

The exciting sport of jetskiing at Montego Bay

10 miles east of Port Antonio, has the biggest waves. You can rent boards here.

TENNIS

Courts are abundant in all the resort areas, as well as Kingston and Mandeville. Every major hotel maintains tennis courts, many lighted for night-time play and many with resident pros. Nonguests can usually play for a fee. Rates for instruction vary.

Kingston boasts the **Eric Bell Tennis Centre**; it hosts the All-Jamaica Open Tennis tournament. The **Montego Bay Racquet Club** *(tel: (809) 952–0200)* features seven floodlit Laykold-surface courts.

WINDSURFING

One of Jamaica's hottest water sports. Most beachfront hotels offer equipment, and instruction comes free for guests, or at a nominal price for nonguests. Most beaches have water sports concession stands – their sales staff will come to you!

WATERSKIING

Negril, with its 7-mile beach, is heaven for this. Many major hotels offer waterskiing free to guests. Even more popular is jetskiing. Waterskis and jetskis are available at water sports concession stands and at hotels throughout the island.

SAVE THE REEFS!

It takes thousands of years for reefs to grow. Yet precious and fragile coral can be destroyed in a moment. The Negril Coral Reef Preservation Society issues the following cautions:
* Do not touch the coral. If you touch or stand on living coral it will die! *Look . . . but don't touch!*
* Do not litter the ocean. Trash is extremely harmful to marine life.
* Do not take or purchase black coral, conch shells, seafans, or starfish. It is illegal to take or purchase coral or tortoiseshell items.
* Do not molest or touch any marine life. Spearfishing is prohibited.

CRICKET

Do not believe anyone who tells you that cricket is the sport of the English. Cricket truly belongs to the Caribbean. In Jamaica it comes close to a national mania. Michael Manley, the former prime minister, even wrote a lengthy book on the subject.

The popularity of cricket bears witness to Jamaica's strong British connections. The colonialists transplanted cricket throughout the British Empire and encouraged the game as part of a policy of breeding an affinity for the culture of the "mother country." In his book *Beyond a Boundary*, C L James claimed that one of the most comforting signs of Jamaica's readiness for self-rule was the island's zeal for the rules and sportsmanship of cricket.

The game that in England gives way to soccer in winter is a year-round sport in Jamaica. Round any corner or crest any hill, even in the most rural backwater, and you are likely to come across a village cricket match in progress, or young people practicing their batting strokes and "googlies" with makeshift bat and ball.

When the English and Jamaican cricket teams meet at Kingston's Sabina Park the whole island seems to erupt in excitement. The greatest triumph in the cricketing season is when Jamaica bests its former motherland – a result Jamaicans regard as a given.

Jamaicans are masters of the idiosyncracies and

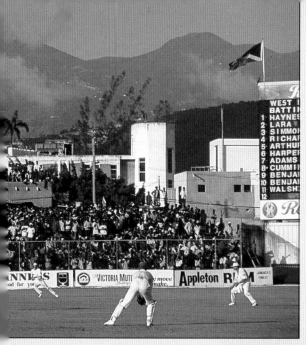

West Indies v England at Kingston's Sabina Park in 1994

held from January to August at Kingston's Sabina Park, the grand shrine of cricket. Then Sabina Park is packed to the gills, and families set up picnics. Enthusiastic roars wash down from the stands, where copious amounts of Jamaican rum and Red Stripe beer are thirstily imbibed.

subtleties that make cricket so complicated for foreigners to understand. The island has sired many of the world's finest cricketing impresarios: Alf Valetine, Lawrence Rowe, "Collie" Smith.

The greatest of all Jamaican cricketing legends is George Headley, the modest cricketing genius born in Panamar. He is Jamaica's "Black Bradman" and, during the 1920s and 1930s, averaged a test century every four innings. He remains the inspiration for thousands of youngsters for whom a distinguished cricketing career is an avenue for social advancement.

Cricket matches – "curry goat" matches – between club teams are usually held on weekends. International and interisland matches are normally

"Cricket, lovely cricket": Jamaicans are wild about it

Food and Drink

Jamaica is a Garden of Eden of fresh produce, and cooking is one of the island's most joyful arts. Jamaica's uniquely zesty cuisine, a fusion of many ethnic traditions, offers a cornucopia of palate-tickling pleasures.

One of the pleasures of eating in Jamaica is dining on a terrace overlooking the sea. Another is sampling the spice-rich local cuisine. Most other international cuisines are represented, particularly in cosmopolitan Kingston. Food quality varies from bad to magnificent and so do service and price, though not necessarily in direct correlation.

Virtually anywhere on the island you will pass by roadside stands selling "jerk" – pork, chicken, or even lobster marinated in thyme, allspice, and Scotch bonnet pepper and cooked over pimento wood so that the meat is saturated with flavor. You will never forget the first fiery morsel of jerk that detonates in your mouth!

Most Jamaican hotels offer guests a chance to taste local temptations like mackerel "run-down," escovitch fish served with festival bread, or curried

goat, and ackee with codfish. Basic roadside restaurants are atmospheric places to sample simple Jamaican dishes not found on most hotel menus: "bammie," a toasted, pancake-flat spongy bread made from cassava; Manish water, a soup (said to be an aphrodisiac) made from tripe and offal; and rice and peas (kidney beans), the island staple – often called the "Jamaican Coat of Arms" – seasoned with onions and coconut milk.

You also will find plenty of restaurants that take pride in their white-glove service and romantic, candlelit ambience. Many of the best restaurants are associated with the deluxe hotels. Here imaginative chefs are introducing newly popular ingredients like squash and fennel into Jamaican recipes dating back centuries. The result is a cross-cultural, home-grown Jamaican *nouvelle cuisine* that is emerging with pride.

If you simply *must* have fried chicken or a burger and fries there are plenty of US-franchised fast-food places and local facsimiles. Locally made hamburgers are usually spiced.

You can top off your meal with Blue Mountain coffee and maybe a smooth rum liqueur, such as Tia Maria. Countless are the bars where you can enjoy hearty rum cocktails: perhaps a Hummingbird or a Blue Mountain Cocktail or Zombie. Jamaica's favorite beer is Red Stripe, the local brew known

Jerk pork and chicken, served everywhere at stalls like this, are a favorite Jamaican snack as "Jamaica's Policeman."

The following chart gives an indication of restaurant price. The $ sign represents the cost of a three-course meal without wine.

$ under $8
$$ under $15
$$$ under $25
$$$$ over $25

KINGSTON

The capital city boasts restaurants from Lebanon to Korea, all run by Jamaicans. Some of the island's finest restaurants are here.

Blue Mountain Inn ($$$$)

The ultimate in casually elegant dining in Kingston. The mountainside inn has a dining terrace overlooking the Mammee River. A French-accented menu has as its inspiration Jamaica tradition – the result is a superb expression of contemporary Caribbean cuisine. A fireplace wards off the evening chill. Reservations required.
Gordon Town Road, 20 minutes from New Kingston (tel: (809) 927–1700).

Chelsea Jerk Centre ($)

Authentic local eatery, selling jerk chicken or pork in a big, sky-blue room with tables and benches.
7 Chelsea Avenue (tel: (809) 926–6322).

Cleo's ($)

Looks like a lean-to with a tin roof and outdoor seating; authentically Jamaican with a large local clientele.
Kingsway Avenue, off Hope Road.

Coffee Terrace Restaurant ($)

Inexpensive lunch spot overlooking the courtyard of Devon House; offers salads, sandwiches, quiches, and patties.
Devon House, 26 Hope Road, Kingston (tel: (809) 929–7063).

Devonshire Restaurant ($$$)

Alfresco dining in the tropical garden of historic Devon House. Surf-'n'-turf (steak and lobster) and gourmet European dishes highlight the menu.
Devon House, 26 Hope Road, Kingston (tel: (809) 929–7046).

El Dorado ($$$)

A favorite eatery for Kingston's business executives, diplomats, and visitors who enjoy its club-like atmosphere.
Terra Nova Hotel, 17 Waterloo Road (tel: (809) 926–9334).

Bar selling the ubiquitous Red Stripe beer and "festival" (fried dumplings)

Jade Garden ($$$$)

Up-scale locals choose this elegant and thoroughly contemporary restaurant for consistently good Chinese cuisine.
Sovereign Centre, 106 Hope Road, Kingston 6 (tel: (809) 978–3476).

Port Royal Grogge Shoppe ($$)

Offers shady outdoor dining at historic Devon House. Food with a *nouvelle* Jamaican touch: ackee crêpes, roast suckling pig, and baked crab backs.
Devon House, 26 Hope Road (tel: (809) 929–7027).

Sir Henry's ($$$)

Excellent for Sunday brunch, with fabulous views over Kingston Harbour from the outside dining terrace. Popular with Kingstonians. Typical are grilled lobster in season, jerk pork, and other Jamaican specialties.
Morgan's Harbour Hotel, Port Royal (tel: (809) 924–8464).

THE EAST
Bamboo Grill Room ($$)

An open-air thatched restaurant (setting for the movie *Cocktail*) serving local and continental cuisine, with views over Dragon Bay.
Dragon Bay Resort, 6 miles east of Port Antonio (tel: (809) 993–3281).

DeMontevin Lodge ($$)

Noted for its delicious Jamaican food – ackee and codfish, mackerel run-dung, curried goat, and so on. Wednesday nights feature a Jamaican buffet ($$$) with live entertainment.
Fort George Street, Port Antonio (tel: (809) 993–2604).

Navy Island ($$)

Perfect for inexpensive sandwich/salad lunch and a priceless harbor view from the dockside restaurant.
Navy Island, Port Antonio (tel: (809) 993–2667).

Rafter's Rest Restaurant ($$)

Watch the rafters arrive as you dine at the edge of the Rio Grande River. A reasonable selection of local specialties, plus international favorites.
Rio Grande Rafting Centre (tel: (809) 993–2778).

If mid-meal munchies strike, head to **Daddy D Snack Centre** ($) on West Street for spicy meat and curried vegetable patties; or the **Mandala Restaurant** ($), near the Roof Club disco on West Street, serving Creole chicken, steam fish, or fish and coconut. For dessert you'll pay but a few pennies for snack cakes and cocoa buns at the **Coronation Bakery** ($).

Boston Bay is where Jamaica's commercial jerk legend began; buy some paper-wrapped "jerk" from the roadside stands ($) and settle down on the wide crescent of white sand. You will need plenty of Red Stripe beer to counteract the eye-watering sauce!

THE NORTH COAST
Almond Tree Restaurant ($$$)

Popularly acclaimed. The huge menu runs from hamburgers, seafood, and fettucine to pepperpot, pumpkin soup, and saltfish, and ackee. Dinner is served by candlelight al fresco on a terrace overlooking the sea.
Hibiscus Lodge, Main Street, Ocho Rios (tel: (809) 974–2676).

Double V Jerk Centre ($)

The town's best "jerk" chicken, pork, or

lobster slow-cooked over pimento wood and served in puddles of sinus-searing sauce for pocket change.
Main Street, Ocho Rios.

Evita's ($$$)
Jamaican–Italian has found the perfect home at Evita's, where authentic pasta dishes are served on the veranda of an 1860 gingerbread house overlooking the bay. The "Rasta Pasta" is a must!
Ocho Rios (tel: (809) 974–2333).

The Little Pub ($$)
A touristy favorite that specializes in surf-'n'-turf (steak and lobster). Serves breakfast, lunch, and dinner with live cabaret-style entertainment.
The Little Pub Complex, 59 Main Street, Ocho Rios (tel: (809) 974–2324).

Old Pimento Restaurant ($$$)
Dine on the terrace or in the intimate Wedgwood Room of this beautiful old Great House. Contemporary Caribbean dishes – ackee and cho-cho strudle with lime butter, bouillabaisse Caribe, for example – are delicious. Desserts are a forte. The staff dresses in 1920s period costume. Sunday champagne brunch is a bargain.
Harmony Hall, 4 miles east of Ocho Rios (tel: (809) 975–4478).

The Ruins Restaurant ($$$)
Built around an old sugar factory with seating around a Bali Hai-like lagoon facing a spectacular waterfall. Cuisine combines Jamaican with Asian.
Da Costa Drive, Ocho Rios (tel: (809) 974–2442).

Seafood Giant ($)
Superb local seafood dishes, such as roasted jackfish with spinach, braised garlic shrimp, and curried Creole garlic lobster.
Runaway Bay (tel: (809) 973–4801).

Shakey's Pizza Restaurant ($)
Pizzas, hamburgers, submarine sandwiches, and salads for fast-food freaks. Yes, they will deliver.
Main Street, Ocho Rios (tel: (809) 974–2716).

Upton House on the Green ($$$$)
Chefs conjure up Caribbean cuisine with a French accent at this wonderful plantation-style restaurant at the Sandals Golf and Country Club.
Sandals Golf and Country Club, Ocho Rios (tel: (809) 974–5691 or (809) 975–0181).

Typical food stand in Montego Bay

JAMAICAN CUISINE

Spice is the life of Jamaican cooking. Allspice constitutes the backbone. Its source is pimento, an indigenous berry that combines the flavors of cinnamon, clove, and nutmeg. Allspice was a favorite ingredient of the Arawak Indians, and Jamaica's contemporary cuisine owes much to the techniques of the early culture—combined with flavorful. Spanish and African highlights. To this exotic palette were added English and Indian influences, and the spices they favored: ginger, black pepper, cinnamon, and nutmeg.

One of the most famous uses of pimento is as "jerked" pork, Jamaica's delicious own finger-lickin' barbecue. The meat is marinated in an incendiary mixture of island-grown spices; then cooked to mouthwatering perfection over a smoking fire of pimento wood in a scrubbed-out oil drum. It is served straight from the coals, wrapped in paper. The Maroons perfected this cooking technique.

Pepperpot soup, too, can pack a wallop. This old Arawak recipe is based on callaloo, a sort of spinach, with okra, salt beef, pig tail or ham hock, and coconut meat, shallots, vegetables, and

the inevitable spices thrown in for good measure. If the gumbo-like broth is not hot enough try adding some pickapeppa sauce, made from mangoes, onions, pepper, raisins, tamarinds, and tomatoes.

Other zesty island dishes include curried lobster, curried goat, peppered shrimp (a delicacy of the Black River area), fresh oysters blended with vinegar and pepper, Solomon Grundy (pickled herring or mackerel), and escovitch fish fried in red pepper, onions, and vinegar.

Jamaican cuisine bears a colorful lexicon. "Dip-'n'-fall-back" is a salty stew made of bananas and dumplings. "Stamp-'n'-go" is a fried, salted codfish fritter. "Run-down" is mackerel spiced and cooked in coconut milk, served as a breakfast dish.

Jamaica's vegetables are mostly humble. To feed the slaves cheaply, breadfruit was brought from the South Seas. From Africa came yams and ackee, whose starchy, yellow-lobed fruit (poisonous when unripe) is cooked to release its toxins; then eaten roasted, boiled, or fried. Ackee looks and tastes rather like

Just some of the huge variety of good things to eat and drink in Jamaica

Green bananas also are boiled and served as a vegetable. Cho-cho (a squash-like vegetable also known as christophine) and pumpkin are other steadfast staples, served on the side, boiled and mashed with butter.

Jamaicans rarely end a meal without fruit or a uniquely named

scrambled eggs. Served with onions and salted codfish, it makes the popular breakfast dish from the Harry Belafonte lyric, "ackee, rice, salt fish is nice."

island dessert, such as "matrimony," a marriage of green or purple star apples with pulped oranges and grapefruit in condensed milk.

THE WEST

Together Mo'Bay and Negril proffer a full platter for every taste and budget. Negril in particular is blessed with budget eateries. In addition to the restaurants listed below Cosmo's, Pamela's Country Restaurant, Paradise Yard, and De Buss all provide Jamaican cuisine at very reasonable prices.

Chicken Lavish ($)

Local Jamaican cooking comes no better. Curried goat, lobster, and red snapper specialties, plus mouthwatering spiced chicken.
West End Road, Negril (tel: (809) 957–4410).

Desi's Dread ($)

This popular budget eatery features "pot-style" dishes based on the Rastafarian philosophy of vegetarian I-tal foods.
West End Road, Negril.

The Diplomat ($$$$)

Seafood and steaks are staples of this elegant, romantic restaurant in a palatial mansion, with a spectacular view of the town and harbor. Special Jamaica dinner of the day.
Queen's Drive, Montego Bay (tel: (809) 952–3353).

Georgian House ($$$)

Very romantic ambience, with 18th-century surrounds and the warm glow of candles. Dishes include barbecued shrimp, lobster Newburg, and freshwater snapper in filo pastry.
Corner of Union Street and Orange Street, Montego Bay (tel: (809) 952–0632).

Gold Unicorn ($$)

Popular with tourists and locals who savor oysters, conch, roast pork loin, lobster thermidor, and Jamaican specials.
7 Queen's Drive, Montego Bay.

Lady Diane's ($$)

Health-food addicts are well served with dishes like vegetable soup, cold tofu salad, brown rice, tempeh shish kebabs, jarame noodle salad, and mango pudding.
Negril Beach.

LTU Pub

Small, down-to-earth cliffside bar with a fabulous mural of an underwater scene, plus a wide range of burgers, fish and chips, and chicken bombay.
West End Road, Negril.

Negril Yacht Club ($)

Surprisingly Chinese food highlights the fare at this beachside bar and restaurant
West End Road, Negril.

The Pelican ($$)

One of Mo'Bay's most popular restaurants, serving Jamaican dishes, such as stuffed cho-cho with rice and peas, curried goat.
Gloucester Avenue, Montego Bay (tel: (809) 952–3171).

Rick's Café ($$$)

Sophisticated décor and a wide-open terrace for sunset and starry-night dining right on the cliff face. Sample dishes include Pompano Jack fillet, conch steak, mixed charbroiled fish platter, linguini bolognese, curry shrimp, and countless exotic desserts.
West End Road, Negril (tel: (809) 957–4335).

Sugar Mill Restaurant ($$$$)

New Caribbean cuisine and a 200-year-old waterwheel combine. Superb food (home-smoked marlin, island pumpkin soup, Creole chicken and lobster) is

Dine alfresco at the classy Rick's Café in Negril

served on an alfresco dining terrace. *Half Moon Golf Club (tel: (809) 953–2314)*.

Tamboo Inn ($)
Magnificent two-story bamboo-and-thatch beachfront restaurant serving inexpensive Jamaican breakfasts and nine types of pizza.
Negril Beach (tel: (809) 957-4282).

Town House ($$$$)
One of Mo'Bay's most atmospheric restaurants is housed in the cellar of a 1765 red-brick house. Steamed snapper, stuffed lobster, and barbecued spare ribs are staple fare. Jamaican specials daily. All dinners are served with a baked potato and large green salad.
16 Church Street, Montego Bay (tel: (809) 952–2660).

Troy and Felix's Serious Chicken Restaurant ($)
Great down-to-earth ambience and colorful décor matched by curried chicken, peppered shrimp, pepperpot steak, and other Jamaican specialties. Cool!
West End Road, Negril.

Zulu's Bar and Eatery ($$)
Tantalizing seafood, grilled steaks, ribs and chicken, and plentiful atmosphere at this streetside restaurant and bar.
Gloucester Avenue, across from Doctor's Cave Beach.

THE SOUTH COAST
Astra Country Inn and Restaurant ($$)
Traditional Jamaican fare with a hint of Italian; the restaurant regularly collects culinary awards. Friday is barbecue night.
62 Ward Avenue, Mandeville (tel: (809) 962–3265).

Bill Laurie's ($$$)
This leading Caribbean steakhouse has a fabulous view of Mandeville, plus a display of antique cars. Quality steak, pork, and lamb chops are done to order.
Bloomfield Gardens, Mandeville (tel: (809) 962–3116).

Yabba Restaurant
Consistently good Jamaican fare is matched by a romantic ambience – you dine on a terrace overlooking the Caribbean.
Treasure Beach Hotel, Treasure Beach (tel: (809) 965–0110).

RUM

Rum is synonymous with Jamaica, the first Caribbean island to produce the liquor commercially. Few dispute that Jamaican rum is the best in the world.

Traditional Jamaican rums – the "Bordeaux of the Caribbean" – are dark and full-flavored. However there are as many grades of rum as ways of enjoying it. Jamaican rums range from rich, aromatic dark rums to Jamaica's famous "overproof" white rums, the strongest of all. Jamaica's 151-proof variety is fondly described as "Jamaica's favorite poison."

White rum is mostly the drink of the local Jamaican. The common islander drinks it straight, chased down with water or coconut milk, accompanied in bars by the loud "bang" of dominoes. Kulu kulu, the "whitest" of white rums,

has seeped into folk medicine and religious ceremony. Rastafarians even steep their *ganja* (marijuana) in the potent elixir.

Rum from its earliest days has been associated with life on the high seas. Sailors and pirates lent it fame, as portrayed by Robert Louis Stevenson in *Treasure Island* ("Yo, ho, ho and a bottle of rum!"). The English purchased rum on a large scale, much of it to serve the needs of the Royal Navy.

Rum is one of the purest of alcohols. It is distilled directly from sugarcane without any need for the preliminary malting required to convert starch to sugar, as in other alcoholic beverages. Hence rum retains more of its natural flavor than other liquors. Many distillers still use the original process developed by Spanish colonists and age their rums in oak casks anywhere from 3 to 20 years. The type of cask lends its own coloration and flavor to the rum.

Those Jamaican rums that have been aged in barrels for over a decade are often so mellow that their subtle taste and delicate aromas can give the smoothest cognac a run for its money.

No one knows where the word comes from. Some say that "rum" is derived from the botanical name for

It's a rum do in Jamaica all right!

sugarcane, Saccharum officinarum. Others suggest it originates from "rumbullion," a word that English planters in the Bahamas used to describe the escapades it induced.

Just as rum is one of the oldest of drinks (the early Spanish first manufactured it by distilling the sweet liquor from molasses, the heavy residue of sugarcane processing), rum punch is one of the oldest cocktails. It originated during the heyday of the sugar plantations, when English planters refined the recipe of "sour, sweet, strong, and weak" (one part lime juice, two parts sugar, three parts rum, four parts water or fruit juice).

Hotels & Accommodations

*Y*ou have a world of choice. Jamaica has the largest selection of accommodations in the Caribbean – everything from lively beach resorts throbbing with reggae and old-style plantation resorts with starched linen and candelabras to mountain inns so quiet that tree frogs sing you to sleep.

Jamaica has over 19,000 hotel rooms, and something for every budget. Many of its resorts are world class – certainly among the best in the Caribbean (several hotels of the rich and famous offer some of the best bargains going). Jamaican hoteliers pioneered the popular "all-inclusive" concept (see page 177), and Jamaica is now fostering the growth of a new, less traditional style of resort far from the beaches – dilapidated old Great Houses are being restored to haughty grandeur for paying guests.

Mid-December to mid-April is high season; consider going in low season, when rates are heavily discounted.

Thomas Cook Holidays lists a complete range of accommodations from "Classic Collection" to "All-Inclusive" in its **Worldwide Faraway Collection** brochure, available from Thomas Cook agencies or their reservations department *(tel: UK (0733) 332255; USA (617) 868–9800)*. The **Jamaica Hotel and Tourist Association** *(JHTA), 39 Gloucester Avenue, Montego Bay (tel: (809) 952–2854)* can provide further information. In the USA **TravelJAM**, *1449 Lexington Avenue, Suite 3a, New York, NY 10128 (tel: 1–800–554–7352)*, acts as a hotel reservation service.

BUDGET HOTELS

Montego Bay and Ocho Rios are not known for budget accommodations. Nevertheless all resort areas have inexpensive guest houses; Negril has many options. Budget accommodations – mountain chalets, family guest houses, and small hotels – are the norm off the tourist path. The famous **DeMontevin Lodge** *(tel: (809) 993-2604)*, an architectural gem in Port Antonio, exudes jaded old-world charm.

BUSINESS HOTELS
(See **On Business**, pages 178–9).

CAMPING AND CABINS
(See **Practical Guide**, page 181)

COUPLES-ONLY RESORTS
All you need is each other. That is compulsory at these exclusive, totally all-inclusive, deluxe hideaways reserved exclusively for couples. Two companies dominate the scene: the Sandals Resorts chain and SuperClubs, which invented the concept. Their renowned rivalry has been a driving force in setting standards of quality throughout the Caribbean. It also has fostered a long list of "firsts" – satellite TV and king-size beds in all rooms, scuba diving and waterskiing as inclusions, and specialty gourmet restaurants, for example. Couples-only resorts offer lots of social activity, from volleyball games on the beach to toga parties, masquerade nights, and cabaret shows.

Sandals has six "Ultra-Inclusive" couples-only resorts in Montego Bay,

Ocho Rios, and Negril. *For worldwide information and reservations contact Unique Vacations (tel: 1–800–SANDALS, or 0171 581 9895 in the UK).* **Couples**, in Ocho Rios, is one of five SuperClubs marketed as "Super-Inclusives." *For information call (tel: 1–800–859-SUPER, or 0181 900 1913 in the UK).*

DELUXE RESORTS
Perched atop their own secluded bays are some of the finest resort hotels in the Caribbean, with opulence and white-gloved service on tap to live up to every brochure-induced expectation. Most date from the 1950s, when Jamaica was one of the first Caribbean destinations to welcome tourists (wealthy tourists). Several have their own golf courses.

Some are old-fashioned in an unfastidious sort of way.

Options for enjoying the genteel lifestyle include:
Tryall Golf, Tennis and Beach Resort, 12 miles west of Montego Bay.
Half Moon Club, 3 miles east of Montego Bay.
Round Hill, 5 miles west of Montego Bay.
Jamaica Inn, Ocho Rios.
Trident Villas, 2 miles east of Port Antonio.
Good Hope Great House, 6 miles south of Falmouth.

It must be difficult to concentrate on eating with this view to look at

INNS OF JAMAICA

The **Jamaica Tourist Board** publishes the free *Inns of Jamaica* booklet listing thirty-eight small hotels and inns. Contact JTB offices worldwide. Some sit high above a photogenic paradise; others are close to the action. US-based **Vacation Network** *(tel: (800) 423–4095 in the US or (312) 883–5140 in Jamaica)* has a "Fly-Drive Jamaica" package combining car rental with vouchers for inns islandwide – excellent for flexible travel.

SPAS

Jamaican vacations can be easily combined with health pursuits. Larger up-scale resorts feature swimming pools, Jacuzzis, exercise rooms, and, occasionally, a cold plunge, steam, and sauna. Most, too, feature exercise and health classes and massage. The most comprehensive is **Swept Away** *(tel: (809) 957–4061)* in Negril, which features a 10-acre sports complex.

At the time of writing, the **Royal Court Hotel and Natural Health Retreat** *(tel: (809) 952–4531)* in Montego Bay was the island's only health-dedicated resort. In Ocho Rios the **Sans Souci Spa and Resort** *(tel: (809) 974–2353)* offers restorative treatments, using mineral spring water for swimming and soaking, massages, paraffin treatments, and mud baths. The **Milk River Mineral Bath Hotel** *(tel: (809) 924–9544)* and **Bath Fountain Hotel** *(tel: (809) 982–2132)* are dowdy and cater to a mostly local clientele.

VILLAS

More than forty percent of Jamaica's accommodations is self-catering. Villas are popular islandwide and range from the quaint and cosy to the palatial, from

Self-catering at Trident Villas, Port Antonio

ALL-INCLUSIVES

Jamaica was the pioneer of the all-inclusive resort vacation, which has swept the Caribbean in recent years. All-inclusives now account for thirty percent of hotel rooms in Jamaica. They also enjoy the highest occupancy rates on the island and are particularly popular with North Americans.

"All-inclusive" means that your indulgences are totally "on the house." Once you enter the gates you can leave your wallets and your budget at home. Everything is usually included in the price, including meals, drinks, water sports, and social activities. Dominating the scene are Sandals and SuperClubs, which together have eleven resorts on Jamaica (see **Couples-only Resorts**). They pioneered the concept and continue to lead the way. Superclubs' Boscobel Beach is also open to families. There also are excellent independent resorts, such as Cibony and Swept Away. A wide range of accommodation, has jumped on the all-inclusive bandwagon. In the process they have diluted the concept, and all may not be as it seems. Many so-called "all-inclusives" have hidden charges, or have reduced choice of facilities.

Family fun at Superclub's Boscobel Beach

the mountain enclave to the beachside gem. Villas are generally staffed with a housekeeper (who can double as a nanny) and cook, and often a gardener. Some villa owners have agreements with resorts that allow guests to use resort facilities. Several of Jamaica's finest resorts also offer villa rentals on-site.

For a listing of villas, apartments, condominiums, and cottages contact the **Jamaica Association of Villas and Apartments** (JAVA), *PO Box 298, Ocho Rios (tel: (809) 974–2508; in the USA call (800) 221–8830); in the UK call (071) 486 3560)*, which publishes a free villa guide, available through JTB offices worldwide. JAVA procures reservations through JAVA Reservations, Inc.

Villawise offers villas in the Ocho Rios region. In the USA contact **Villas and Apartments Abroad** *(tel: (800)*

433–3020) or (212) 759–1025.

Jaw-dropping options in Port Antonio include **Goblin Hill Villas** *(tel: (809) 993–3286)*, a lush private estate at San San Beach; **Crystal Cove** *(tel: (809) 925–8108)*, a superb three-bedroom villa where your cook can examine the catch delivered by fishers to your personal dock; and **Trident Villas and Apartments** *(tel: (809) 993–2602)*. Even more luxurious are the villas of **Tryall Golf, Tennis and Beach Resort** *(tel: (809) 956–5660)*, west of Montego Bay.

On Business

*J*amaica has a thriving business community centerd in Kingston, the commercial capital. The island also plays host to conventions and meetings lured by balmy weather, superb facilities, and a panoply of postbusiness activities.

Jamaica's economic development agency, **Jamaica Promotions Ltd**, acts as the coordinating agency for business ventures between local and overseas private companies. JAMPRO promotes investment and assists investors. *For information contact JAMPRO, (JAMPRO), 35 Trafalgar Road, Kingston 5 (tel: (809) 929–7190)*.

Similarly the **Jamaica Chamber of Commerce**, *85a Duke Street, Kingston (tel: (809) 922–0150)*, promotes, fosters, and protects commerce and industry.

Most business offices and factories are open Monday to Friday, 9am–5pm. Very few offices are open on Saturday.

ACCOMMODATIONS

There are two major hotels close to Kingston's business center – the Jamaica Pegasus and the Wyndham New Kingston – (see Conference and Exhibition Facilities below). The **Oceana Hotel and Conference Centre**, *3 King Street, Kingston 10 (tel: (809) 922–0920)*, is conveniently located next to the Kingston Conference Centre.

BUSINESS ETIQUETTE

Jamaicans are not big on ceremony or formality. Hence while business suits are advised, they are not *de rigueur*; you may find your Jamaican business partner prefers casual (but usually chic) clothing.

COMMUNICATIONS

Hotels with convention facilities have fully fledged business centers; most other major hotels have telex, fax, and photocopying services. EHC Industries Ltd, 22–4 Island Life Centre, *6 St Lucia Avenue, Kingston 5 (tel: (809) 968–8000)*, supplies **audio-visual systems**. Computer Business Systems Ltd *(tel: (809) 929–5180)* and Innovative Systems Ltd, *106 Hope Road, Kingston 6 (tel: (809) 978–3512)* can supply a wide range of **computer services**. Contact Technology Plus Ltd, *8 Balmoral Avenue, Kingston 10 (tel: (809) 926–6997)*, for **electronics**.

CONFERENCE AND EXHIBITION FACILITIES

Jamaica is growing in popularity as a meeting and convention spot and has a wide variety of facilities able to handle business meetings both large and small.

Every office of the Jamaica Tourist Board has a designated group travel specialist to help facilitate meetings and incentive travel. The JTB's Kingston headquarters has a group and convention department. **ITCS Incorporated Ltd**, *22 Trafalgar Road, Kingston 10 (tel: (809) 978–4732)*, offers conference services.

Kingston

The **Jamaica Conference Centre**, opened in 1973, is conveniently located in the heart of Kingston's commercial district. It features eight meeting rooms, the largest of which seats 1,050, and 2,400 square feet of exhibition space. *For information contact the Jamaica Conference Centre, 14–20 Port Royal Street, Kingston*

(tel: (809) 922–9160).
The **Jamaica Pegasus Hotel**, *81 Knutsford Boulevard, Kingston 5 (tel: (809) 926–3691)*, has convention facilities for up to 1,000 delegates. The **Wyndham New Kingston**, *77 Knutsford Boulevard, Kingston 5 (tel: (809) 926–5430)*, can accommodate up to 1,000 banquet-style, 1,300 theater-style.

Ocho Rios
The elegant 289-room **Ciboney Ocho Rios** *(tel: (809) 974–1027)* has a beach, water sports, and full resort facilities. The spectacular 720-room **Jamaica Grande Renaissance Resort** *(tel: (809) 974–2201)* is Jamaica's largest convention hotel; it can accommodate 2,700 people.

Montego Bay
The beachfront **Wyndham Rose Hall Resort** *(tel: (809) 953–2650)*, just outside Montego Bay, is a major meetings hotel with a 7,500-square-foot ballroom. **Tryall Golf, Tennis and Beach Resort** *(tel: (809) 956–5660)* is perhaps Jamaica's most exclusive resort.

EXHIBITIONS
An annual trade exhibition – **EXPO** – is sponsored each March in the National Arena, Kingston, by the Jamaica Manufacturers Association and the Jamaica Exporters Association. *For information contact PRO (tel: (809) 926–6740)*. **JAPEX**, Jamaica's annual travel trade exhibition, is held each May at the Jamaica Grande, Ocho Rios. *For information contact Jamaica Tourist Board offices worldwide.*

MEDIA
The Daily Gleaner (tel: (809) 922–3400) contains a business section. Caribbean Publishing Ltd, *18 West Avenue, Kingston 8 (tel: (809) 925–3228)*, publishes the **Caribbean Business Directory** and **Caribbean Basin Commercial Profile**, which provides statistics, regulations, and other useful titbits. Another local publication is **The Investor's Choice** *(tel: (809) 929–2993)*.

Business topics on Jamaica and other Caribbean destinations also are covered by *Caribbean Week*, published in Barbados; *Caribbean Today*, published in Trinidad; and *Caribbean Update, 52 Maple Avenue, Maplewood, NY 07040 (tel: (201) 762–1565)*.

SECRETARIAL SERVICES
The Jamaica Tourist Board's group travel specialist can help facilitate secretarial services and equipment. The following Kingston-based companies provide secretarial and ancillary services: **Express Typing and Photocopying Centre**, *9 Lilford Avenue, off Old Hope Road (tel: (809) 929–9720)*; **Placement and Business Services Ltd**, *35 Constant Spring Road, Kingston 10 (tel: (809) 926–8359)*; and **Personnel Services Ltd**, *40 Shortwood Road, Kingston 8 (tel: (809) 924–0533)*. See the Yellow Pages for additional sources.

TRANSLATION SERVICES
English is the national tongue, as well as the language of commerce. **ITCS Incorporated Ltd**, *22 Trafalgar Road, Kingston 10 (tel: (809) 978–4732)*, can provide translating and interpreting conference services if needed.

MISCELLANEOUS
AC Marine International Ltd, *81 Hagley Park Road, Kingston 10 (tel: (809) 929–1726)* acts as **Customs brokers and import and export license consultants**. See also Yellow Pages.

Practical Guide

CONTENTS

ARRIVING

By Air

Most tourists arrive by air at Donald Sangster International Airport, 2 miles east of downtown Montego Bay; others arrive at Norman Manley International Airport, 13 miles by road south of downtown Kingston. In either case you face a long walk from your plane to the immigration hall (at the time of writing a new terminal was under way at Donald Sangster International Airport).

Brace yourself for the sea of people that mills outside. There will be no shortage of hustlers waiting to hurry you into a taxi or private shuttle bus. Major resorts provide a shuttle service for pre-booked guests. Visitors on organized package tours will be met on arrival. Car rental agencies have booths outside the arrival hall, as does the Jamaica Tourist Board. The Jamaica Union of Travelers Assocation (JUTA) has representatives at the airport and cruise ports and can arrange ground transfers upon arrival.

A direct (nonstop) scheduled service is available to Jamaica from England and other points in Europe and from several North American gateways. Charter operators offer additional direct services. Scheduled flights also are available from a variety of South American countries and other islands in the Caribbean. At the time of writing the national airline, Air Jamaica, was in the process of being privatized.

A departure tax of J$400 is payable in Jamaican currency or the equivalent in US dollars, pounds sterling, German Deutchemarks, or French francs at the airport when leaving. The departure ounges at Donald Sangster and Norman Manley airports have the usual wide range of duty-free shops, banks, and snack bars.

By Boat

Jamaica is a popular stop on itineraries of several cruise companies (in 1992 it received 654,000 cruise arrivals).

The island has deep-water ports in Kingston, Montego Bay, Ocho Rios, and Port Antonio. Montego Bay handles approximately twenty-five percent of cruise ship arrivals and has five berths, plus a modern terminal building. Ocho Rios is favored for day stops and has three deep-water piers, with capacity to handle mega-liners. Port Antonio can handle smaller ships. Kingston, the seventh largest port in the world, is hoping to re-establish itself as a port of call.

Immigration

UK citizens require a passport and a return or onward ticket. US and Canadian citizens need proof of citizenship (passport or original or certified birth certificate) and return or onward ticket. No visa is required. Visitors are allowed to stay for 6 months. An application to extend your stay must be made to the Ministry of National Security and Justice, *Kingston Mall, 12 Ocean Boulevard, Kingston (tel: (809) 922–0080)*.

Many European and Canadian citizens take excursions to Cuba from Jamaica (see **Getting Away from It All**, pages 134–5). US citizens are prohibited from spending dollars in Cuba, though not from traveling there (Cuban authorities do not stamp your passport). Canadians and Europeans do not need visas; tour companies can arrange visas for US citizens.

CAMPING

No camping facilities are currently recommended by the JTB, and there are few established camping facilities. You will find plenty of tent space and cabins on the beach at Negril and a few sites along the coast outside other major resorts. Some beaches do not allow camping. The Blue Mountains have several sites for hikers and campers. The best known is **Maya Lodge and Campground**, headquarters of the **Jamaica Alternative Tourism, Camping and Hiking Association** (JATCHA), *PO Box 216, Kingston (tel: (809) 927–2097)*. This private marketing group represents more than 4,000 beds and campsites in "Alternative Tourism."

CHILDREN

Jamaicans love children, and the country is generally safe. Great care should be taken to prevent sunburn and insect bites. Use caution at waterfalls and where coral is present. Kingston has the Bustamante Hospital for Children *(tel: (809) 926–5721)*. (See also **Children**, pages 154–5.)

CLIMATE

Jamaica is a tropical island with consistently hot, humid weather all year round. On the north coast constant breezes mollify the heat and humidity so that the climate feels balmy. The average annual temperature on the coast is 82 °F (28 °C); temperatures vary between 81 and 90 °F (27 and 32 °C).

Temperatures in the highlands average 10 degrees Fahrenheit lower and are positively salubrious, like an eternal spring. The Blue Mountains, however, are much cooler. The south coast is generally hot and moderately dry, even semi-arid in parts.

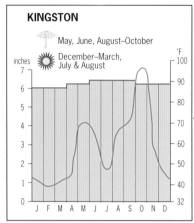

KINGSTON

May, June, August–October

December–March, July & August

inches / °F

WEATHER CONVERSION CHART
25.4mm = 1 inch
°F = 1.8 × °C + 32

Use common-sense caution. Most theft is opportunistic. Do not carry valuables or jewelry, and carry only as much money as you need – keep the rest locked in a hotel safe. Do not leave items in view in a vehicle, and always lock car doors. At public beaches valuables left unattended are subject to theft. Petty thefts also occur on public transportation. Verify the identity of anyone who knocks unexpectedly at your hotel room before opening the door. (See also **First Steps**, page 20.)

Portions of Kingston are on occasions subject to curfew. Avoid ghetto areas at all times.

Use only licensed taxis.

At the time of writing the Jamaica Tourist Board was establishing a call-free "Crime Stoppers" hotline to solicit information on crime.

Rainfall averages 78 inches, with marked regional variation. Tropical showers can occur year-round, most often at night. The bulk of the rain falls between May and June and from September to November. The northeast coast receives three times more rain than the rest of the island.

CONVERSION CHARTS
See opposite.

CRIME
Jamaica is a poor country and some islanders feel forced to make a living "scuffling" as petty thieves. Handguns are in wide circulation, and there are occasional reports of tourists being mugged on the street or robbed at gunpoint in their hotel rooms. Such incidents occur relatively infrequently, although crime has shown a marked upturn in Jamaica in recent years.

CUSTOMS REGULATIONS
Jamaica's incoming duty-free allowance is 25 cigars, 200 cigarettes, 1 pint of liquor (except rum), 1 pound of tobacco, and 1 quart of wine. All fresh flowers, plants, honey, fruits, meats, and vegetables (except canned) are restricted.

US Customs allows $400 of duty-free imports every 30 days. Personal allowances for visitors 21 years or older include 200 cigarettes, 100 cigars (Cuban cigars are illegal), plus one liter of wine or spirits. Many Jamaican-made products are exempted from duty, regardless of value.

UK citizens are allowed 200 cigarettes or 50 cigars; 2 liters of wine; 1 liter of spirits; 60cc/ml of perfume; plus £32 of gifts, souvenirs, or other goods.

It is important to note that importation of illegal drugs or animal or plant products is subject to severe penalties.

Conversion Table

FROM	TO	MULTIPLY BY
Inches	Centimeters	2.54
Feet	Meters	0.3048
Yards	Meters	0.9144
Miles	Kilometers	1.6090
Acres	Hectares	0.4047
Gallons	Liters	4.5460
Ounces	Grams	28.35
Pounds	Grams	453.6
Pounds	Kilograms	0.4536
Tons	Tonnes	1.0160

To convert back, for example from centimeters to inches, divide by the number in the the third column.

Men's Suits

UK	36	38	40	42	44	46	48
Rest of Europe	46	48	50	52	54	56	58
US	36	38	40	42	44	46	48

Dress Sizes

UK	8	10	12	14	16	18
France	36	38	40	42	44	46
Italy	38	40	42	44	46	48
Rest of Europe	34	36	38	40	42	44
US	6	8	10	12	14	16

Men's Shirts

UK	14	14.5	15	15.5	16	16.5	17
Rest of Europe	36	37	38 39/40	41		42	43
US	14	14.5	15	15.5	16	16.5	17

Men's Shoes

UK	7	7.5	8.5		9.5	10.5	11
Rest of Europe	41	42	43		44	45	46
US	8	8.5	9.5		10.5	11.5	12

Women's Shoes

UK	4.5	5	5.5	6		6.5	7
Rest of Europe	38	38	39	39		40	41
US	6	6.5	7	7.5		8	8.5

DRIVING

Accidents

After an accident do not move vehicles or allow them to be moved. Remain at the scene until a police officer arrives; have someone else call the police. Jamaicans can be excitable. Do not allow yourself to be drawn into an argument. If you have a camera take a photo of the scene. Obtain the name and address of anyone involved in the accident, as well as the make and license number of vehicles. Record any other pertinent information, including the names and addresses of witnesses. Inform your rental company as soon as possible.

Breakdown

Car rental companies provide an emergency telephone number to call in the event of breakdown. Most have 24-hour emergency service. Off the beaten track locals will offer their services as mechanics. The Yellow Pages lists automobile repair services.

Car Rental

All the major international companies (Avis, Budget, Dollar, Hertz, National) operate in Jamaica. Rental car agencies have desks in major hotels and at Montego Bay and Kingston airports. Car rental charges can give you a shock – Jamaica is one of the most expensive places in the Caribbean. Dozens of local firms offer more competitive rates. Largest and among the least expensive is **Island Car Rentals**, *17 Antigua Avenue, Kingston 10 (tel: (809) 926–8861)*, with offices throughout Jamaica. Other companies are listed in the Yellow Pages. Rates begin at about $65 a day, during low season.

It is wise to make your reservations in advance, as certain classes of vehicles may not be available upon arrival. If you enjoy the sun consider a convertible Jeep. You must be 24 years of age to rent a car in Jamaica, with a valid driver's license and major credit card.

About ten categories of vehicle are available, including minivans and Jeeps. Automatics are widely available, though a manual is recommended. Automatics do not have the versatility required in Jamaica, where potholes and kamikaze chickens appear out of nowhere and precision gear changes are often called for. You may wish to rent an air-conditioned car – this will cost you extra.

Cars with driver can be rented from the **Jamaica Union of Travelers Association** (JUTA): $70 to $160 a day.

Motor scooters and motorcycles can be rented from roadside offices in all the major resorts from $17 a day.

Distances/Driving Time
Montego Bay to Negril 50 miles/1½ hours
Montego Bay to Ocho Rios 62 miles/1½ hours
Montego Bay to Mandeville 72 miles/2 hours
Ocho Rios to Port Antonio 60 miles/2½ hours
Ocho Rios to Kingston 60 miles/2 hours
Kingston to Mandeville 65 miles/1½ hours
Kingston to Port Antonio 68 miles/2 hours
Kingston to Negril (via Mandeville) 149 miles/4 hours

Documentation
A foreign driver's license is required and is valid for up to 3 months. International Driver's Permits are not needed in Jamaica.

Gas
Gas stations are located throughout the island. Gas is sold by both the liter and the gallon – cash only, no credit cards. Many gasoline stations are closed on Sunday.

Insurance
Car rental fees cover driver's insurance. Collision Damage Waiver insurance is offered by rental agencies; without it you will be assessed damage up to a minimum of $500. Before leaving home check to see whether your existing car insurance covers you. Some credit cards also provide pre-existing coverage for international car rental. Carefully scrutinize the car before accepting it; check for pre-existing damage (including scratches and dents) and to see that items shown on the checklist are actually functioning.

Speed Limits
The speed limit is 30mph in towns and villages; 50mph on main highways. In general Jamaicans drive fast, often recklessly fast considering local conditions. Watch for passing vehicles.

ELECTRICITY
The standard electricity supply is 110 volts/50 cycles; 220 volts is available in some hotels. Large hotels can supply adaptors as needed. Many rural homes have electricity.

EMBASSIES AND CONSULATES
Australian High Commission, *64 Knutsford Boulevard, Kingston 5 (tel: (809) 926–3550)*.
British High Commission, *26 Trafalgar Road, Kingston 10 (tel: (809) 926–9050)*.

Canadian High Commission, *Royal Bank Ltd Building, 30 Knutsford Boulevard, Kingston 5 (tel: (809) 926–1500)*. **US Embassy**, *Jamaica Mutual Life Centre, 2 Oxford Road, Kingston 2 (tel: (809) 929–4850)*.

EMERGENCY NUMBERS

Air-Sea Rescue: 119
Ambulance: 110
Fire: 110
Police: 119

Thomas Cook travelers' checks loss or theft: 0044 733 502995 (24-hour service, reverse the charges).

GAMBLING

Horse racing takes place every Wednesday and Saturday and public holidays at Kingston's Caymanas Park. Several larger hotels have slot-machine casinos with electronic blackjack. The Jamaica Grande Hotel, Ocho Rios, has the largest. Otherwise there are no casinos.

HEALTH

No vaccinations are required to enter Jamaica. Standards of health are generally high. All tap water in Jamaica is purified and filtered. It is wise to wash all fruit and vegetables.

Sunburn is a potential problem. Do not underestimate the strength of the tropical sun. Use sunblocks!

Most large hotels have a resident nurse. There are public and private hospitals in all major towns – all have 24-hour emergency facilities. Smaller towns have health clinics and doctors' offices (see Yellow Pages under "Physicians" for listings). Check your personal insurance before leaving home to avoid additional expensive premiums in Jamaica.
Falmouth: Falmouth Hospital *(tel: (809) 954–3250)*.

Kingston: Bellevue Hospital *(tel: (809) 928–1380)*; Kingston Public Hospital *(tel: (809) 922–0210)*.
Mandeville: Mandeville Hospital *(tel: (809) 962–2067)*.
Montego Bay: Cornwall Regional Hospital *(tel: (809) 952–5100)*.
Ocho Rios: St Ann's Bay Hospital *(tel: (809) 972–2272)*.
Port Antonio: Port Antonio General Hospital *(tel: (809) 993–2646)*.

HITCHHIKING

Hitchhiking is a way of life for Jamaicans. Schoolchildren, for example, typically hitch between school and home. If driving you will be waved down for a ride all along your route. If hitching stretch your arm out and wave your hand up and down to attract a ride.

INSURANCE

Travel insurance to cover unforeseen medical expenses and loss of property is highly recommended. Consider purchasing cancellation insurance to protect against the cost of unused travel services in the event that you must cancel your trip. Driver's insurance is included in the cost of car rental (see Car Rental above).

LANGUAGE

English is the official language; the local dialect (*patois*) is widely used (see also **First Steps**).

LAUNDRY

All major hotels have laundry service; villas usually have maid service. Self-service launderettes also are available in major tourist resorts. In villages and outlying regions it is possible to find local women who will wash your clothes for a small fee.

MAPS

A good road map is essential. The Jamaica Tourist Board publishes a free 1:356,000-scale *Discover Jamaica Road Map*, available from tourist board offices worldwide; car rental companies normally provide a free copy. Thrifty Car Rental publishes *Vacation Jamaica Visitors' Map and Guide*. Texaco publishes a 1:30,000 topographical road map showing locations of Texaco gas stations. Both maps feature detailed town maps on the reverse. Some larger hotels also stock a smaller *Road Map Jamaica*, free to guests.

MARRIAGE

Something about the tropical heat and romance of a Caribbean vacation induces many visitors to marry in Jamaica. Tying the knot is a civil ceremony. You must have been on the island for 24 hours and possess a birth certificate (those under 21 need a letter of parental consent) and divorce or death certificates if divorced or widowed. Hotels can make all the arrangements. Most require you to send notarized copies and photocopies of passports 6 weeks in advance. Tour operators usually provide full details of necessary documentation, and a package is the cheaper and easier way to arrange an island wedding. Otherwise apply to the Ministry of National Security and Justice, *12 Ocean Boulevard, Kingston; (tel: (809) 922–0080)*. For a religious ceremony contact clergy in advance.

MEASUREMENTS

Jamaica uses imperial weights and measures.

MEDIA

Leading newspapers include *The Daily Gleaner* and *The Herald* morning dailies and *The Star*, an afternoon tabloid. *The Observer* is published on Wednesday and Friday. *The Gleaner* also publishes a weekly tourist guide. The Jamaica Tourist Board publishes a quarterly *Tourism Talk*. *The Vacationer* is a free weekly newsletter.

The following foreign newspapers and magazines are widely available: *The Times*, *Daily Telegraph*, *Miami Herald*, *New York Times*, *Wall Street Journal*, and *USA Today*.

There are two AM radio stations (JBC and RJR) and eight FM radio stations (JBC, FAME, KLAS, LOVE, Power 106, WAVES, RJR, and IRIE). Interference is frequent and reception intermittent. The BBC World Service is broadcast.

There are two television stations, JBC/TV and CVM Television. Local newspapers publish TV guides. North American cable channels are available in most larger hotels.

MONEY

Bank hours are Monday to Thursday, 9am–2pm, and Friday, 9am–3pm or 9am–noon, 2:30pm–5pm. A few banks open on Saturday. Official currency is the Jamaica dollar (J$), divided into 100 cents. Bills are issued in denominations of J$1, J$2, J$5, J$10, J$20, J$50, and J$100. Coins are: 1c, 5c, 10c, 20c, 25c, and 50c.

The exchange rate is subject to daily fluctuation. There is no limit to the amount of foreign currency you may bring in. It is illegal to change foreign currency except at banks, hotels, and other authorized dealers. A commission is charged for converting currency. Thomas Cook travelers' checks can be cashed free of charge at the Thomas Cook representative: Grace-Kennedy Travel Ltd, *19 Knutsford Boulevard, Kingston 5 (tel: (809) 929–6290)*.

Foreign currency may be used to pay for hotels, car rentals, duty-free shopping, and so on (check whether the prices you are being quoted are in US or Jamaican dollars). There is no sales tax. US dollars are acceptable for most purchases, as are Thomas Cook travelers' checks. Major credit cards are accepted in hotels and most restaurants and stores.

Western Union can arrange a telegraphic money transfer. In Jamaica call (800) 991-2056 toll-free, or (809) 926-2454 in Kingston.

NATIONAL HOLIDAYS
New Year's Day (1 January)
Ash Wednesday Variable
Good Friday Variable
Easter Monday Variable
Labor Day (23 May)
Independence Day (1st Monday in August)
National Heroes Day (3rd Monday in October)
Christmas Day (25 December)
Boxing Day (26 December)

OPENING HOURS
Most offices and factories open Monday to Friday, 9am–5pm. Stores generally open Monday to Saturday, 8:30am–5pm, with ½-day closing on Wednesday or Thursday. Some stores in tourist resorts stay open 7 days a week, including early evening. Museums and tourist sites vary; see individual entries.

ORGANIZED TOURS
Dozens of local tour companies offer day and multiday excursions. For sightseeing services inquire at hotel desks or with the Jamaica Tourist Board.

In Kingston Grace-Kennedy Travel Ltd, _19 Knutsford Boulevard, Kingston 5_

(tel: (809) 929–6290), can assist with sightseeing. Pleasure Tours _(tel: (809) 925–5584)_ and Galaxy Tours _(tel: (809) 931–0428)_, with offices islandwide, offer a wide range of excursion tours. In Montego Bay VC Tours Ltd, _40 Union Street, Montego Bay (tel: (809) 979–5213)_, offers such tours as "Montego Bay Highlight" and "Negril Experience."

A growing number of locally based tour companies offer tours for special-interest travelers. Sense Adventures, _Box 216, Kingston 7 (tel: (809) 927–2657)_, offers natural history tours, canoeing, and hiking programs. It also can arrange caving, bicycling, horse trips, and other adventure activities. The Touring Society of Jamaica, _Salt Gut, Boscobel PO, St Mary (tel: (809) 975–7158)_, offers birding, art study, and natural history tours.

PHARMACIES
Pharmacies can be found nationwide. All standard medicines and toiletries are available. Hours of opening vary widely. Many pharmacies stay open until 9pm weekdays and are open Sundays. Consult the Yellow Pages.

PLACES OF WORSHIP
Jamaica has more churches per capita than any other country in the world. Most religious denominations are represented. The only synagogue is in Kingston. Churches are listed in the Yellow Pages.

POLICE
The police speak English and are generally helpful. The police in Montego Bay, Negril, and Ocho Rios have special tourism liaison officers. Special uniformed "tourism assistants" were introduced in the main resort areas in 1994. For emergency assistance dial 119.

POST OFFICES

Every town has a Post Office. The reception desks at most hotels sell postage stamps and will accept letters and postcards for mailing. Some also will handle packages (charges can be added to your bill). Allow a minimum 1 week for delivery to Europe or North America.

PUBLIC TRANSPORTATION

Public transportation is not one of Jamaica's strong points. The Jamaican Railway Corporation was disbanded in 1992; a train service no longer operates.

Airlines

Jamaica has one domestic airline, Trans-Jamaican. It operates daily service between Kingston (both Tinson Pen and Norman Manley International), Montego Bay, Port Antonio (Ken Jones), Ocho Rios (Boscobel), and Negril (Negril Aerodrome). Trans-Jamaican utilizes nineteen-seater, twin-engine Dornier 228s (and smaller aircraft for eight persons).
Kingston *tel: (809) 923–8680.*
Montego Bay *tel: (809) 952–5401.*
Negril *tel: (809) 957–4251.*
Ocho Rios *tel: (809) 975–3254.*
Port Antonio *tel: (809) 993–2405.*

Buses

Local bus services connect all villages and towns. However service is disorganized, and buses are overcrowded. Schedules are flexible. In Montego Bay the Montego Bay Municipal Bus Company has a service at the airport and the hotel strip just east of Rose Hall.

Minibuses are the cheapest, and most crowded, way to get around (J$2–J$5 virtually anywhere). Outside towns they can be flagged down. Contact the Tourist Board for departure points in town.

Taxis

Taxis ("called contract carriages") are widely available. In Kingston some taxis are metered, but not elsewhere. Taxis have prescribed charges between given points, although few drivers adhere to this. Negotiate a price before you get in (consult your hotel concierge beforehand for appropriate rates). Licensed taxis display red PPV plates (Public Passenger Vehicle); other taxis are unlicensed and should be avoided.

The Jamaica Union of Travelers Assocation (JUTA) operates special tourist taxis and buses, including ground transfers. Prices are controlled. Contact the following offices for rates and reservations:
Falmouth *tel: (809) 954–2684.*
Kingston *tel: (809) 926–1537.*
Montego Bay *tel: (809) 952–0813.*
Negril *tel: (809) 957–4200.*
Ocho Rios *tel: (809) 974–2292.*
Port Antonio *tel: (809) 993–2684.*

SENIOR CITIZENS

Few concessions are offered for senior citizens. Seniors' travel clubs in your home country may offer special tour packages. In Jamaica Pleasure Vacation Tours *(tel: (809) 924–1471)* offers a senior citizens' excursion.

TELEPHONES

Direct telephone service with the rest of the world operates 24 hours a day. Most up-scale hotels have a direct-dial service, though charges are often excessive. Coin-operated public telephones are widely available, and instructions are posted. If using a calling-card do not give the number to anyone but a telephone operator. Service is irregular, reception sometimes erratic.

Rates for international direct-dialed

calls are cheaper 6pm-5am daily and on Sundays. AT&T USADirect Service to the USA is available from select hotels and many telephones islandwide. From hotels call 872; or for reverse charge (collect) calls from other phones call *(800) 872-2881*. The operator can place your call and bill your AT&T account.

For operator assistance call 112 (domestic) or 113 (international). Telephone directories are issued in bedrooms (the Yellow Pages follows British alphabetization). For directory assistance call 114.

International Codes

Australia: 61
USA and Canada: 1
United Kingdom: 44

Boatphone *(tel: (809) 462-5051)* offers cellular phone rental. You also can link your cellular phone to their service.

Faxes and telex can be sent from most hotels or the local branch of JAMINTEL, the nation's telecommunications company. Cables and telegrams can be sent from most Post Offices.

TIME

Jamaica is on US Eastern Standard Time; GMT less 6 hours (spring/summer); GMT less 5 hours (autumn/winter). Daylight Saving Time is not observed.

TIPPING

Most hotels and restaurants add a ten to fifteen percent service charge. If not tip according to quality of service. All-inclusive resorts do not allow tipping.

TOILETS

There are virtually no public facilities. Most large hotels have restroom facilities.

TOURIST OFFICES

The Jamaica Tourist Board promotes tourism and handles information. They can provide general information, maps, plus an information vacation guide.
Head Office: *ICWI Building, 2 St Lucia Avenue, Kingston 5 (tel: (809) 929-9200).*
Montego Bay: *Cornwall Beach (tel: (809) 952-4425).*
Ocho Rios: *Ocean Village Shopping Centre (tel: (809) 974-2582).*
Negril: *9 Adrija Plaza (tel: (809) 957-4243).*
Port Antonio: *City Centre Plaza (tel: (809) 993-3051).*

Offices Abroad

UK: *1-2 Prince Consort Road, London SW7 2BZ (tel: (071) 224-0505).*
USA: *801 Second Avenue, New York, NY 10017 (tel: (212) 856-9727).* Regional Offices: Chicago *(tel: (312) 527-1296);* Dallas *(tel: (214) 361-8778);* Los Angeles *(tel: (213) 384-1123);* Miami *(tel: (305) 665-0557);* New York *(tel: (212) 856-9727).*
Canada: *1 Eglinton Avenue East, Suite 616, Toronto, ONT M4P 3A1 (tel: (416) 482-7850).*

Thomas Cook Group Representative

Grace-Kennedy Travel Ltd, *19 Knutsford Boulevard, Kingston 5 (tel: (809) 929-6290).* Thomas Cook Holidays has a separate representative, details of which are given to clients before departure.

TRAVELERS WITH DISABILITIES

Jamaica is not well set up for travelers with disabilities. Many newer resort hotels have been designed with facilities that take into account the needs of the disabled. Streets and pavements are uneven and there are no ramps. Many resorts are at both beach and street level.

ACKNOWLEDGEMENTS
The Automobile Association wishes to thank the following photographers and libraries for their assistance
in the preparation of this book.
LEE ABEL 133, 152b, 153a, 153b, 153c; ALLSPORT (UK) LTD 162/3, 163b (A Murrell); ARDEA LONDON
LTD 80/1, 81; MARY EVANS PICTURE LIBRARY 12, 12/13, 13a, 13b, 130; NATURE PHOTOGRAPHERS LTD
80 (K J Carlson); PICTURES COLOUR LIBRARY LTD 92, 151; REX FEATURES LTD 17b; D SAUNDERS 1,
99; SPECTRUM COLOUR LIBRARY 98, 177; TRIP 152a (D J Francis).
The remaining pictures are held in the Association's own library (AA PHOTO LIBRARY) and were taken by
Jon Wyand with the exception of the following pages which were taken by R Victor 24, 25, 41b, 101, 103,
111b, 114, 135, 140, 141, 143, 144b, 145b, 155, 159b, 161, 164, 168b, 169a and 171.

CONTRIBUTORS
Series adviser: Melissa Shales   **Copy editor:** Ron Hawkins   **Verifier:** Kate Patrick   **Designer:** Design 23
Indexer: Marie Lorimer